Moving to Maine
THE ESSENTIAL GUIDE TO GET YOU THERE

MOVING TO MAINE

THE ESSENTIAL GUIDE TO GET YOU THERE

Victoria Doudera

DOWN EAST BOOKS
ROCKPORT, MAINE

To Matt, Nate, and Alexandra—all shining parts of Maine's bright future. And to Ed, my partner in our Maine adventure.

Copyright © 2000 by Victoria W. Doudera
Cover illustration © 2000 by Scott Earle
ISBN 0-89272-479-X
Book design by Janet L. Patterson
Printed and bound at Versa Press, East Peoria, Ill.

5 4

Down East Books
P.O. Box 679, Camden, ME 04843
Book orders: 1-800-766-1670

LIBRARY OF CONGRESS CATALOGING-IN-PUBLICATION DATA

Doudera, Victoria, 1961–
    Moving to Maine: the essential guide to get you
    there / by Victoria Doudera.
          p. cm.
    Includes index.
    ISBN 0-89272-479-X (pbk.)
    1. Maine—Guidebooks. 2. Moving, Household—
Maine—Handbooks, manuals, etc. I. Title.
F17.3 .D68 2000
974.1'044—dc21
                         00-43130

Contents

Introduction

This is a book about the state fondly known as "Vacationland." It's designed for people who are thinking about moving to Maine at some point in the near or distant future. It should prove useful as well to folks who have recently arrived—maybe even to people who have lived here a lifetime.

Nearly forty thousand people, young and old, will move to Maine this year, for as many reasons as there are lobster pots in Penobscot Bay or potatoes in an Aroostook field. An unsurpassed natural environment, a lifestyle that encourages a slower pace, a low rate of crime, and an economy that values creativity and entrepreneurship are just some of the lures. Affordability is another.

Bill and Allie Lou Richardson of Islesboro moved to Maine by pure chance. "We wanted to retire on the water," says Allie Lou. "And it was the only area we could afford at the time. We love the easy pace of life here, the clean air and natural beauty. And we love tying our boat up where we can see it!"

Whether you are retiring like the Richardsons, relocating to pursue a better way of life, or simply dreaming about what it's like to live Down East, chances are you've already begun to ask yourself some questions:

- Is Maine part of mainstream America?
- Are there good-paying jobs up there that offer rewarding work?
- Can I live in a remote, rural state?
- Will my business still prosper?
- Is there enough cultural and ethnic diversity? Is there any?
- Are there decent doctors? Schools? Restaurants?
- Can I survive the winter?
- Will my family find things to do?
- Will I ever really fit in?

If any of these questions sound familiar, then read on. Here is the scoop on what it's *really* like to live in Maine. The biggest advantages. The surprising benefits. And even the pitfalls. With loads of useful information, helpful hints, and tips from those who've already blazed the trail, you'll learn how to manage in Maine *before* the boxes are packed and the moving van's loaded.

Perhaps you've already made your move and become a resident of the Pine Tree State. If so, welcome! Use this book as a guide to your adopted home. You'll find all you need to get acquainted, including tips on everything from registering your car to rafting your first North Woods river.

No doubt you've been here before, visiting like millions of others do every summer. You've likely come to appreciate the state's beauty—the rough-hewn coastline and rugged islands, the spruce-filled forests and towering mountains, the clean rivers, lakes, and streams. And you probably guess that the same attributes that make Maine "Vacationland" make it a beautiful place to call home.

But vacationing in Maine is one thing: living here is another kettle of cod altogether.

To begin with, there are Mainers themselves. What are they really like as friends and neighbors? Are they gruff and remote as the stereotype suggests? Can someone from out of state ever hope to become a part of the community?

It might surprise you to know that, despite their brusque image, Mainers are some of the most helpful, hospitable people around. "I've never met a general population of more open and friendly people," says Mary Griffin, who moved to Orono in 1996 from Charleston, South Carolina. "I've made friends here in Maine that I know I'll have for the rest of my life."

Brad Rourke, a former Californian, agrees. "We didn't choose Maine; Maine chose us. We came here for a job opportunity, having never set foot in the state. We were prepared for the stereotypical New Englanders—tight-lipped and terse. Instead we've received a warm welcome and made fast friends with a good cross-section of folks."

What is it that draws you here? The relaxed pace? The natural beauty and views? The lack of billboards?

"I automatically shift into low gear the minute I cross the border into Maine," says Dorothy Paradis, who moved to Cornish several years ago. "I love wearing shorts and sandals to work, seeing lots and lots of green, and making my own rules, hours, and goals."

My Story

Like many others who move to Maine, I was disillusioned with climbing the corporate ladder and I was tired of subways, smog, and the suspicious-looking beetles that skittered around my Boston apartment. I longed for a clean, natural environment and a less hectic lifestyle. I imagined hiking, sailing, and skiing right outside my front door.

My soon-to-be-husband Ed wanted a lifestyle change, too. He was tired of the urban bustle, but he did not want to live "in the boonies." A city boy at heart, he needed a place with some activity: good restaurants, maybe a movie theater or two, and a YMCA. He planned to start a law practice and contribute to the community—ideally at the same time. Sailing was another priority.

Neither of us knew a single soul in Maine. Not only that, we'd visited the state only once together. Yet that one time had made a deep impression. Maine seemed like the right place for the kind of life we envisioned.

One raw January day in 1986 we set out in Ed's aging sports car, headed north. We wove our way up the coast, feeling like explorers on a thrilling expedition. Since we possessed neither jobs nor trust funds, it seemed like a good idea to buy a business—an inn or a restaurant maybe. That day we toured several turn-key properties, but it was a forlorn Victorian, smack on Route 1, that captured our interest. Beneath the house's grime and through the myriad cobwebs, we spied ornate plaster moldings and peeling tin ceilings, lovely old floorboards, and deep parlor fireplaces. Underneath it all we could see a lovely inn. As we stood shivering in the damp chill, that mysterious alchemy between old homes and romantic souls worked its magic, and we succumbed to the Victorian's hidden charms. Three months later our Maine adventure had begun.

We barely had time to think about our new lives that first year. Renovating the house took months of sawdust and sweat, and then we were thrust headlong into the role of innkeepers. Ed baked muffins and flipped flapjacks, and in his spare time he passed the Maine Bar Exam. He opened a law practice in a pretty tin-ceilinged room at the front of the inn. We joined town boards and the church down the street, adopted a black lab puppy, and began to feel at home.

Yet it wasn't long before we noticed there were palpable differences to living in Maine, differences that went beyond the physical surroundings.

One day I was running some errands in the village. As I slowed at a blinking yellow light at one of the few intersections, a car horn began honking insistently at me. In a flash, my Boston-driver instincts kicked in. "Give me a break," I muttered. I scanned the streets for the offending car, ready to give its obviously obnoxious driver a nasty look, at the very least. There, idling on a side street, I found the culprit: an enthusiastic woman I'd met the day before, smiling and waving while sounding her horn.

These are the kinds of stories newcomers tell all the time, the kinds of tales that demonstrate the unexpected richness of life in Maine. When Ed and I fell under the spell of that old house years ago, we really became part of a place with much more to offer than we could have ever imagined. A place with people—some of them "natives" and some (like us) "from away"— who've become good friends. A state where our children are valued members of the community. A place where I really can hike, sail, and ski practically in my backyard. Personally, I couldn't agree more with the tourist slogan— Maine *is* "the way life should be."

Nevertheless, the nation's most northeasterly state is not for everyone. Living in the more remote sections or weathering the sometimes long winters can be a challenge. Taxes can seem comparatively high and ethnic diversity disappointingly low. Maine isn't perfect, although some of us consider it a lot closer to perfection than many other places.

This Book

In writing *Moving to Maine,* I spoke with new residents who've moved here from all over the United States within the past few years. These kind souls shared their biggest challenges and rewards as new Mainers. "What do you wish you had known before you moved here?" I asked. Their thoughtful responses to my many questions helped me enormously in creating what I hope is a truly useful, informative guide.

In this book I give a broad overview of the state, with as much specific information as possible on key topics like tax rates, medical centers, and schools. Where I have not provided specifics, I've given you the path to find them. For instance, Chapter 7 lists a few of the state's better-known golf courses, along with a way to research the remaining one hundred or so. In many cases, I've directed readers to a website. I'm sure many of you agree that the Internet is an excellent way to research an area, and Maine in particular has an overwhelming amount of quality information online, including several superb sites like the State of Maine home page (www.state.me.us). For the more traditional researcher, I've included phone numbers. Chances are, a real person will pick up the phone, and nine times out of ten that person will be both helpful and polite.

Timeliness and accuracy have been my goals; but please forgive me if I've omitted something or if information has evolved since publication. Even in Maine, things do change.

If you care to share your input for further editions, I would love to hear from you. Please write me care of Down East Books, P.O. Box 679, Camden, ME 04843, or send me an e-mail at vdoudera@midcoast.com. I welcome and thank you for your comments.

Moving anywhere is an undertaking that requires courage, energy, creativity, and faith. I wish you all of these as you discover life in Maine.

The Allure of Maine

"I believe the essence of Maine is independence and integrity, and a sense of community that is being lost in other parts of the country."
—GEORGE MITCHELL*

Before I actually moved here, I knew very little about Maine. Although I had canoed down the Saco River and fished in Rangeley Lake, I thought of the state in a stereotypical way: a vast expanse on top of New Hampshire, full of moose, lobsters, and folks who muttered "Ayuh." Maine seemed too big and too wild to have its own distinct identity.

I settled in Maine and soon discovered—as do all newcomers who don't know it already—that Maine is a place apart. I'm not talking about the scenery, although the lighthouses and spruce-covered islands are nothing short of spectacular. Nor am I referring to the wildlife on land or sea for which the state is famed. I'm describing the soul of Maine, something that is felt more than seen. An attitude, a mystique, summed up in the sigh that escapes the lips when crossing the Piscataqua River at Kittery, regardless of how many times you've done it before.

The Essence of Maine

There is a palpable Maine spirit, no matter where in the state you go, a mixture of pride and perseverance sprinkled with independence and old-fashioned neighborliness. Mainers have "moxie," a term from the late 1800s meaning nerve and verve (and also the name of a century-old beverage, still popular

---

*Former Senate Majority Leader George Mitchell, of Maine, quoted in *Portland Monthly Magazine*, July 1999.

Down East). Like the state's heroes—Civil War General Joshua Chamberlain, pioneering Senator Margaret Chase Smith, and former Governor Edmund Muskie, to name just a few—Mainers may be humble, but they aren't afraid to stand up for what's right.

Businesspeople who relocate to Maine from other states are often amazed by the strong work ethic here. The sun rises early in the Pine Tree State, and most Mainers have already had a mug or two of coffee before the rest of the country is out of bed. They also are exacting, and believe in quality and workmanship. Whether their field is biotechnology or blueberries, residents here comprise the best workforce in the country.

The Maine spirit creates an indelible impression on those who adopt the state as their home. Many newcomers find the indefinable attitude contagious. Some see it as a precious commodity that might spoil if not tended: "Be prepared to be a part of Maine," advises newcomer Carol Doherty-Cox, who moved to Port Clyde from Westchester County, New York. "Don't bring your old life with you. The value of Maine is in its identity. We don't need to inundate the state with people who want to remake it in their image."

Writers have long looked for words to describe the unique essence of this place. In her 1964 book, *State o' Maine,* Louise Dickinson Rich summed it up this way:

> To Mainiacs, Maine is not merely a place. It is a spiritual home and shelter as perfectly fitting and comfortable and natural as its shell is to a snail; which, like snails, they carry with them wherever they may go. To them, Maine is a state of mind and a way of life inseparable from the geography and topography of the area and from their own bones and blood and thoughts and dreams. It is an element, as necessary to them as water is to fish. It is almost a religion.

Governor Angus S. King, Jr., calls the state's spirit "that indefinable attitude that won't take no for an answer, that says yes to life and its infinite possibilities."

The Maine mindset and lifestyle can come as a bit of a shock to newcomers. The rhythm of life is slower, and the frenetic pace of large cities (and even most suburbs) is not commonly found. "People aren't living off their calendars here," says Thad Chilton, who relocated from outside of Washington, D.C., in 1998. "Nobody pulls out their date book to make an appointment." Catching up on the latest news at the post office is viewed as more important than merely processing people through a line. Cashiers at stores—even large department chains—take time to chat or offer helpful advice about purchases. Newcomers who are used to a faster pace will find that patience is a virtue that can often come in handy here.

Maine is old-fashioned in other ways as well. Deals may still be sealed with a handshake, and issues are often worked out over the backyard fence rather than in the county courtroom. This is not a cynical, world-weary place—honesty and integrity are assumed to be part of everyone's makeup. When I forgot my wallet at a large grocery store shortly after moving here, the store manager handed me a fifty-dollar bill and began walking away. "Don't you want my name?" I asked, incredulous. "That's all right," he said, dismissing me with a wave of his hand. "You'll pay me back."

The ways of the village flavor life even in the urban areas. When in need, Mainers depend on one another. Neighbors drop off fragrant chicken pot pies or hearty casseroles when a new baby comes; community suppers are held to raise money for families struggling with an illness or unexpected accident. This willingness to lend a hand was demonstrated to the rest of the nation during the state's great ice storm of 1998. Crews from as far away

ONLY IN MAINE

Maine towns often appear on lists of the best places in the nation to live. Here are a few examples:

- Portland was chosen as a "North American Dream Town," by *Outside* magazine in 1999.
- Camden was called Maine's best small town by the *Maine Sunday Telegram* in 1997. Cornish came in second.
- Bath was selected as one of the "The 100 Best Small Towns in America," in a 1995 book of the same name.
- Deer Isle was chosen as the country's fifth-best small art town by John Villani in *The 100 Best Small Art Towns in America.* Belfast ranked tenth, and Lewiston came in at ninetieth.
- Brunswick was chosen as one of the top five places to retire by *Money Magazine,* June 2000, (as reported on MSNBC).

15

as North Carolina, here to fix downed lines, were astounded at the warm welcome they received from victims of the storm, many of whom had been without power for several days.

In many ways, the state functions as one big small town. But despite this closeness, newcomers are warmly welcomed.

"We were concerned about being seen as outsiders, especially since that was how we were treated in South Carolina," says Mary Griffin of Orono. "But the Bangor region really welcomed and embraced us and made us feel as though we were part of a great community."

Something for Everyone

Maine's natural assets have always been its greatest attraction to vacationers, and they are a big lure for new residents as well. "One of the biggest advantages to living in Maine is the beautiful natural environment," says

Schooners such as the *Grace Bailey,* built in 1882 to carry lumber, now offer sailing cruises along the coast from May to October. *Photo courtesy of Maine Windjammer Cruises.*

Lynda Chilton, a native of Virginia. "When I go anywhere here, my views are of beautiful mountains, oceans lapping at rocky shorelines, charming old homes, and comfortable farms."

Maine offers something for everyone, largely because of its size. Measuring 320 miles long by 210 miles wide, the state encompasses 33,215 square miles—about as much land area as all of the other five New England states combined. Its famous rocky coastline curves in and out for 3,478 miles, from York to Washington Counties. It comprises 16 counties with 22 cities, 424 towns, 51 plantations, and 416 unorganized townships. One county, Aroostook, is so big that it alone is larger than Connecticut and Rhode Island combined. Distances between Maine towns can be vast for travelers used to the scale of southern New England. For instance, Portland, the state's largest city, is actually closer to New York City (328 miles) than to Madawaska on the Canadian border (356 miles).

Maine boasts 542,629 acres of state and national parks, including Acadia National Park, Baxter State Park, and the ninety-two-mile Allagash Wilderness Waterway. The state's highest peak, Mt. Katahdin, rises almost a mile above sea level, while Acadia's Cadillac Mountain has the distinction of being the tallest mountain on the eastern seaboard.

Water abounds in Maine—on a map the state appears to be sinking, so frequently do blue patches interrupt the green! There are thirty-two thousand miles of rivers and streams, fifty-one lakes that have an area of at least five miles, and, of course, the meandering coastline. More than three thousand islands dot the bays, making for spectacular sailing. Pleasure boats of all sizes ply the waters, as do working lobster and fishing vessels, ferries, and the beautiful historic wooden schooners called windjammers. "For me, spending time on the coast of Maine was truly magic," says Lynda Chilton. "I felt that this place was calling to me and my family."

The People of Maine

Ask new residents in Maine why they like living here, and, without fail, they will mention their neighbors. Mainers (not many people use the term "Mainiacs" anymore) may be gruff or loquacious, natives or relative newcomers, yet almost all of them share a sense of community and a love for their state and its resources.

"People here are friendly and supportive," says Dottie Paradis, who moved to Cornish from Massachusetts in 1999. "Not at all the staunch and rigid Yankees I imagined."

"We also chose Maine for the people, " says Lynda Chilton. "In the little bits of time we spent here, we made good friends. People I would have kept in touch with, even if we hadn't decided to move up. When you live in a metropolitan area, you get used to not having time for close friends, and the people you come in contact with in stores, restaurants, and in business are stressed out, and often surly and rude. Road-rage invades all parts of life. In Maine, people take the time to be nice—you feel you are part of the community."

Approximately 1,244,000 people live in the state of Maine in an estimated 465,000 households. The majority of them call the countryside home; while nearly 80 percent of the population of the United States lives in metropolitan areas, only 35 percent of Mainers live in cities, the major ones being Portland, Bangor, Augusta, and Lewiston-Auburn.

A Cultural Mix

Who lives in here? A 1994 report from the Maine Department of Labor called "Diversity and Community," notes that the state has a slightly higher number of English, Irish, Scotch, Dutch, and German ancestors than the United States as a whole. "The most outstanding feature of ancestral composition in Maine, however, is the large percentage of French," says the report. According to the 1990 census, the French contribution to the population of the United States is 5.9 percent, yet in Maine that percentage is 28.2 percent. "From a national point of view, this large French concentration is unique. Over time the French have shown the least inclination of all other European countries to migrate and have typically had the highest rates of return."

Many of these French Mainers are descendants of the early white settlers who eventually migrated southward from Canada, but those settlers were not the region's earliest modern inhabitants. The Wabanaki Indians, or "People of the Dawnland" were here first. Their tribes include the Passamaquoddies, Penobscots, Maliseets, and Micmacs, and there are still many Native Americans—about 5,600 in various corners of the state.

Mainers are very proud of their ethnic roots, and fairs, festivals, celebrations, and religious observances honor the origins of the state's many cultures. Bagpipes play at the Highland Games in Brunswick, and the lilting sounds of traditional French *chansons* fill the air in Lewiston and Auburn at the Festival de Joie. Midsommar Festival, held in the Aroostook County towns of New Sweden and Stockholm, commemorates that area's Swedish heritage, and a day honoring Maine's Wabanaki tribes occurs in April. Despite these celebrations, almost all newcomers, like Peter Mahncke of Kingfield, feel Maine is still rather homogenous culturally, lacking a blend of cultures, races, and religions.

"I love Maine's beautiful landscape, the slower pace, the tranquility, and the ability to use the land for recreational purposes," notes Mahncke. "The only down side to living in Maine might be that the population isn't very diverse."

Growing Diversity

It's true that the face of Maine is largely white—97.6 percent—although that percentage is slowly changing. It may not appear so, but today the Pine Tree State is experiencing the greatest growth in racial diversity in its history. Between 1990 and 1997, for example, the Asian population grew 25.9 percent, the African-American population 14 percent, and the Hispanic population 24.9 percent. The Census Bureau predicts that this growth will continue, but the pace will be slow.

PROFILE

"I chose the state of Maine because of the skiing, and also because I was offered a good job with Carrabassett Valley Academy," says Peter Mahncke, who emigrated to Kingfield from Germany in 1997. "I think there are many benefits to living here," he says. "The slower pace, the relatively clean environment, the beautiful landscape, the good political leadership, and the balance between the state's economy and ecology are big pluses. And there is little suburbia and low crime, which I also like. If you enjoy living somewhat removed from corporate America and you are not looking for a fast-paced lifestyle with hectic people, this is the place for you."

What about discrimination? It's hard to gauge racial attitudes, and few or no studies have been done addressing the issue. Mainers who are minorities report mixed reactions: some feel comfortable here, while others sense a lack of acceptance.

Kristy Scher moved to Maine with her husband and two sons in June of 1999 and says she sometimes feels "the palpable stigma of being different." She explains: "Being Jewish, we find ourselves in the religious and cultural minority here in the midcoast. We frequently have to explain to people things like our reasons for keeping kosher. That said, there is an active Jewish community in our area, and we have quickly become involved in that."

Most Mainers—no matter what their ethnic origin—believe the state will benefit as diversity grows.

Slow Population Growth

Maine's population on the whole is growing, albeit slowly. Between 1996 and 1997, growth was estimated at .2 percent. (New England's population, by contrast, grew by an estimated .4 percent.) Who's moving in? All kinds of people, really—young families, early retirees, skilled professionals, risk-taking entrepreneurs. They come from all over the map, although migration from southern New England and the mid-Atlantic region outnumbers other spots.

"If I had to rank them," says Valerie LaMonte, the Director of the Center for Real Estate Education at the University of Southern Maine, "I'd say that the most common home states of new residents are Massachusetts, New Hampshire, Connecticut, New York, and Pennsylvania." The "Current Population Survey," a report issued by the Census Bureau that includes data on the annual rate of moving, backs up her informal data. The survey estimates that of the forty thousand or so "in-migrants" to Maine, nearly half were from the Northeast. According to recent reports, about a quarter of Maine's new residents came from the West, and almost as many relocated from the South. Midwesterners moving to Maine are more rare—only about a thousand made the trek in 1997.

The northeastern United States has historically been a source for Maine's new residents. Many Maine towns were settled in the 1700s by families from Massachusetts or New Hampshire seeking cheap land and abundant game. A century later, the so-called rusticators (moneyed summer residents of Bar Harbor, Kennebunkport, Islesboro, and other coastal communities) boarded steamships to escape the heat of their home cities of Philadelphia, Boston, and New York City. And many of their families liked it here so much that they settled in Maine permanently.

What Is a Native?

Some good-natured speculation goes concerning just who is a "native." Strictly speaking, Maine natives have ancestral ties to the state going back at least three generations. It gets confusing because sometimes folks will answer the "Are you a native" question with, "Yep. Born and bred." But to many sticklers, merely being born in Maine isn't enough. Here's the succinct explanation: Just because the cat has kittens in the oven, that don't make 'em biscuits.

It's all in fun, though—after all, folks "from away" have been coming to Maine for centuries. I like the old joke in which the fellow from Massachusetts asks the Mainer, "Have you lived here all your life?"

To which the Mainer answers, "Not yet."

No matter where you live in the state, your neighbors may be from just about anywhere: Veazie or Virginia, Scotland or Scarborough.

A Safer Place to Be

In addition to scenic beauty and welcoming people, Maine boasts something that, unfortunately, few other states can claim: friendly streets and neighborhoods. "We haven't locked our car doors in three years," says Brad Rourke, of Camden, who moved to Maine from southern California in 1997. "We feel safe when we're out with our kids. My internal early-warning radar system doesn't have to be on all the time. In fact, it's funny: every time I see a thriller or mystery at the movies, the setting is usually a gritty, urban environment. When I leave the theater, my city-tough attitude is on, and I look around corners for danger and generally have my bristles out. But then I quickly realize that's unnecessary and laugh at myself."

While law enforcement officials are quick to recommend street smarts even in the smallest town, the fact remains that crime in Maine is tame

CRIME RATE PER 1,000 POPULATION

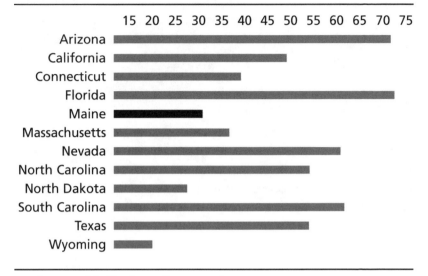

Data provided by *Down East* magazine.

compared with other places. The state consistently ranks among the top ten safest states, and in recent years, Maine has made the top three. According to the Uniform Crime Reports, compiled by the FBI, the 1997 crime rate in Maine—representing everything from petty to violent crimes—was 31.32 offenses per 1,000 people. The 1997 national average was 49.99. Contrast that statistic with those of a few other states (Illinois' rate of 51.41 or Florida's of 72.72), and you get a sense why newcomers feel appreciably more secure in Maine. And the state seems to be only getting safer: in 1998, the crime rate was 30.73 offenses per 1,000 people, the lowest number in more than twenty years.

A Four-Season Climate

Although some might shiver at the very thought of the long winters, there are plenty of people who consider the Pine Tree State's climate to be ideal. "Maine is recognized as one of the most healthful states in the nation," claims the state tourism bureau. Smog-free air and moderate temperatures (average 70 degrees in summer, 20 degrees in winter) benefit residents whether working or playing. "I love the change of seasons," says Elizabeth Burrell, of Rockland. "The weather in California was so predictable."

And what of the legendary winters? While they offer an excellent chance to wear colorful fleece jackets and down parkas while pursuing a wide range of cold-weather sports, winters here tend to be the victims of hazy memory and hyperbole. For the most part, the force of old man winter in Maine has been greatly exaggerated. Data suggest that although the winters are frosty, prolonged severe cold spells are rare. "I find the winters invigorating," says Lynda Chilton, who moved here from Virginia. "Especially because I enjoy outdoor activities in all seasons." (Maine's climate and delightful seasons are discussed in more detail in Chapter 6.)

Lobster for Lunch

Another tasty benefit of life in Maine is the freshness and variety of great things to eat. Food ranges from the simple to the sophisticated, from nouveau cuisine to nostalgic favorites. Restaurants with creative chefs offer new twists on local ingredients like fiddlehead ferns or smoked mussels, as well more traditional fare that changes with the seasons. Ethnic cuisine—once scarce in the state—is increasingly common, even in many small towns.

Of course, Maine is internationally known for its big-clawed crustacean—more than 46 million pounds of lobster are harvested in a typical year. In addition to lobster, the Gulf of Maine is home to mussels, clams, shrimp, scallops, and fish of all stripes. Some varieties you can catch yourself—others can be found at local supermarkets, fish markets, or fresh at the dock.

The classic lobster bake features baked potatoes, corn on the cob, steamed clams, and lobster with plenty of butter. *Photo courtesy of Maine Lobster Promotion Council.*

Tourists may travel here for giant shore dinners, but I'm living proof that you don't *have* to love lobster to live in Maine. If seafood's not your style, markets and restaurants offer just about anything you crave—certified Black Angus beef, organically raised chickens, free-range turkeys, and spring lamb are just a few delicious possibilities. Small farms supply fresh eggs as well as a tempting array of cheeses, vegetables, and fruits. Farmer's markets display items like crunchy greens, fresh corn, and maple syrup, and supermarkets provide a wide variety of local (as well as imported) products and produce.

The changing seasons bring more of Maine's bounty: strawberries, raspberries, cranberries, and tangy little blueberries that thrive in our acidic soil. Come July, it's easy to see why the state produces 98 percent of the country's lowbush blueberries. Apples are another significant crop. Heirloom varieties like tart Northern Spies ripen alongside more common varieties such as Macintosh and Delicious at orchards large and small.

Living in Maine means savoring a whole pantry of delicious foods, including our famous red crustaceans. "I love having a lobster roll for lunch," says Gloria Guiduli, who moved to the midcoast from Massachusetts in 2000. "But I also enjoy the little Japanese take-out stand downtown and the local chocolate factory. Before I moved up, I wondered if finding ingredients for recipes here would be difficult, but I'm able to locate what I need and then some."

2 How Maine Works

> *"Maine should be a quick story—it's not a big or a populous place and nowhere near as old as any comparable site in Europe or Asia. But the historic flavor of this small corner of America needs room for its rich diversity to be explained, to be narrated, even to be sung in bits of poetry and scraps of fiction intermingled with the exposition of facts."*
>
> —Neil Rolde*

How does the Pine Tree State operate? A quick look at the geography and history of the nation's most northeasterly corner goes a long way toward understanding how the state functions on a day-to-day basis.

Maine Geography

Maine is diverse—geographically speaking—thanks to the work of massive glaciers long ago. As the slow-moving masses of ice crawled southeast, they scraped and softened the contours of mountains, gathered loose soil and stones, and broadened and deepened river valleys. When the climate warmed again, beginning fourteen thousand years ago, the glacier unloaded rocks, stone, and soil as it melted, creating moraines, eskers, and drumlins as well as the bodies of water dotting the state. Ancient river valleys were dammed up, forming chains of lakes, such as those in Belgrade. The weight of the mile-thick ice sheet had depressed the land, so when the glaciers melted and sea level rose, water flooded the sunken terrain, forming Maine's bays, inlets, and coves. Today's islands are the hilltops and ridges of this "drowned coast." Because of the glaciers, Maine contains the only fjord on the east

---

*Quoted from *Maine: A Narrative History,* by Neil Rolde. Gardiner, Me.: Tilbury House Publishers, 1990.

MAINE STATE FACTS AND SYMBOLS

Capital: Augusta
Population: Approximately 1.2 million
Gemstone: Tourmaline
Fossil: *Pertica quadrifaria*
Cat: Maine Coon Cat
Insect: Honeybee
Animal: Moose
Flag: The coat of arms of the State of Maine is placed on a blue field of the same shade of blue as in the flag of the United States. Adopted by the Legislature of 1909.
Motto: Dirigo—A Latin term which means "I lead."
Tree: White Pine, adopted by the Legislature of 1945.
Floral Emblem: White pine cone and tassel *(Pinus strobus)*. Adopted by the Legislature of 1895.
Bird: Chickadee *(Parus atricapillus)*. Adopted by the Legislature of 1927.
Fish: Landlocked Salmon

coast—Somes Sound—and even, believe it or not, has its own stretches of "desert" in places like Freeport and Wayne, where erosion has exposed ancient deposits of glacial sand.

When the climate warmed, grasses grew, along with other plants, flowers, and eventually, forests. Animals multiplied, and soon the first Mainers appeared.

A Little History

Prehistoric inhabitants of Maine included Paleo Indians, who lived here perhaps 11,500 years ago. Historians believe they were followed by the Archaic Indians, and finally by the Red Paint People, whose artifacts, colored with distinctive red ochre, have been found on North Haven Island and elsewhere.

Evidence indicates that these natives enjoyed many of the same pleasures that present-day vacationers do. They headed to the coast in the summer for cool breezes and hearty seafood feasts. The middens, or piles of shells, they left behind are remnants of ancient clambakes. In addition to shellfish, they enjoyed porpoise and seal meat—items that have not remained a part of our modern summer menu.

When the first Europeans arrived is still a controversial topic. Debate rages over whether or not Vikings had a settlement in Maine. W. Hodding Carter, trip leader of the 1998 Snorri expedition, which traced the Vikings' route in a replica of a Norse ship, says, "We know for sure they were in Greenland and Newfoundland. We aren't certain they sailed to Maine. But after three months in a replica of a Viking merchant ship, I'm convinced that any self-respecting Viking would have found his way to Penobscot Bay."

An ancient Norse penny found in Brooklin, Maine, adds weight to Carter's sentiments. Dating back to 1065 or so, it's the oldest European artifact ever found in North America. The coin resides at the Maine State Museum in Augusta, although it is currently on display at the Smithsonian Institution.

European Exploration

The first Europeans to "discover" Maine came in search of gold, spices, and the elusive Northwest Passage to the Orient, as well as more practical items such as fish, furs, and lumber. Beginning in 1524, Italian, Spanish, French, and English explorers traded along the coast, sailing home with full cargoes of valuable furs, cedar, and sassafras root, as well as stories of abundant fish and enormous lobsters.

Did the Vikings reach Maine? This eleventh-century Norse coin, found in a coastal Indian archaeological site in Brooklin in 1974, seems to indicate they did. *Photo courtesy of Maine State Museum.*

Maine's first European settlers were a band of eighty Frenchmen, led by Sieur de Monts and Samuel de Champlain. They landed on St. Croix Island in the St. Croix River (notable for having the highest tides in the continental U.S.) in late June of 1604. The area was part of the region known as La Cadie, today called Acadia. After a dreadful winter

27

HISTORIC MAINE FIRSTS

1604	The French explorers who settled on St. Croix island near Calais produce the country's first regularly issued newspaper, The Master William.
1604	This same hardy band stages the first Christmas revelries—complete with wine and feasting—in North America.
1620	The first water power plant in the United States was built on the Piscataquis River in South Berwick.
1641	York becomes America's first chartered city (although Mainers hate to admit it was part of Massachusetts at the time).
1775	First naval battle of the Revolutionary War occurs when Machias rebels capture the British schooner Margaretta.
1851	Maine becomes the first state to prohibit the sale of all alcoholic beverages.
1853	Isaac Winslow, a sailor, is the first to pack canned corn.
1905	The Pastime, the first movie theater in the country built exclusively for the presentation of moving pictures, opens in Brunswick.
1949	Margaret Chase Smith, of Skowhegan, becomes the first woman to be elected to the U.S. Senate.

during which nearly half of the party perished, the Frenchmen pulled up stakes and headed to a more hospitable climate—Nova Scotia.

Throughout the seventeenth century, explorers came and went, including some of the more famous names from New England history, like Captains John Smith and Miles Standish. Smith landed on Monhegan Island in Muscongus Bay in 1614. He made Monhegan his home base for several years, and penned a bestseller about the region's attributes. Smith was the first to refer to Maine and the environs as New England rather than New Virginia, as it was first designated.

Soon the wild mainland bordered by islands came to be known simply as "Maine," and no one has been able to definitively say where the name came from. Some suggest it was derived from the term "mainland," others that it came from a French province. Although few Europeans lived here, the

The craggy cliffs of Monhegan have changed little over the years. The photo above, from the collection of the late Frank Claes, depicts men seining for fish in 1926. Nearly eighty years later, a group of lobstermen head past the same spot. *Both photos courtesy of the Island Institute.*

region was carved into huge tracts of land which were granted to wealthy English noblemen by the King. These land grants remained virtually unpopulated until the mid-1600s, when the successful Massachusetts Bay Colony began expanding, first into New Hampshire, and then northward into the "Province of Maine." In 1641, York, located on Maine's southern coast, became the first chartered city in America.

The hardy families who cleared the land, fished the sea and lakes, and began new lives in Maine were technically part of the colony—and later, state—of Massachusetts. From the beginning, though, their lifestyles and attitudes exhibited the independent spirit that is still strong in Maine. Native Americans, lumberjacks, mill owners, ice cutters, sea captains, fishermen—their colorful stories unfold in museums located throughout the state (see Chapter 8).

Maine remained part of the Commonwealth of Massachusetts until 1820, when papers were signed in Freeport to make it into a separate state. The twenty-third state, Maine came into the Union as part of the historic Missouri Compromise, a turning point in the nation's ongoing debate over slavery. (The "compromise" provided that Maine would be admitted as a free state, balanced by Missouri as a slave state.)

Statehood marked the beginning of another chapter in Maine's history, a story as rich and colorful as a prize-winning blueberry pie. To savor more than this small slice, try historian Neil Rolde's highly readable history, *Maine: A Narrative History,* published by Tilbury House Publishers, of Gardiner, Maine.

A Quick Tour of the State

Maine is divided into sixteen counties. Although the county system is not as significant as town government, a glance at these counties, each of which has a distinct personality, is a good way to learn what's where. To best understand the state—and to get where you're going—you'll need a dependable map. The DeLorme Company's atlases, maps, and guides are known throughout the world for their reliability and quality—many Mainers consider them indispensable, especially the *Maine Atlas and Gazetteer.* Besides showing Maine in painstaking detail, down to the last logging road, the atlas is chock-full of information, from driving distances to state parks and canoe routes. It's available throughout the state at bookstores, supermarkets, and sporting-goods stores, or directly from the Yarmouth company at (800) 452-5931. Drop by their headquarters and see the massive globe *Eartha* or visit their website at www.delorme.com for more information.

ANDROSCOGGIN COUNTY

This south-central county of 105,259 residents is named for the state's third-largest river. Although its waters were once so toxic that the river was said to glow in places, the Androscoggin is now the healthiest it has been in a century and is a prime spot for kayak and canoe enthusiasts, some of whom paddle in the Great Falls Canoe Race held each June.

The Androscoggin winds through the county's two biggest cities, Lewiston, home of Bates College, and Auburn. The friendly burghs are so entwined they share two nicknames—"L-A" and "the Twin Cities"—and they rival Portland in their combined size and economic importance. Auburn is a city of about 23,000 people, while 36,800 or so folks call Lewiston home.

Lewiston and Auburn are bustling centers of commerce and cultural activities, favored by many companies because of their prime location, which is nearly smack in the middle of the most populous part of Maine. Once an industrial area full of mills and factories, which attracted a large French Canadian population, the pair have enjoyed a great rebirth in the late nineties, retrofitting office centers into these old mills and attracting new businesses of all sorts. Though they are bustling, the Twin Cities are ringed with bucolic villages, among them Leeds (population 1,800), Poland (4,500), and Turner (4,700), and they are only an hour or so from the heart of the western mountains. Androscoggin county is also dotted with crystal-clear lakes, ponds, rivers, and brooks, including Lake Auburn. Nearby Lost Valley is a popular ski area once the snow flies.

AROOSTOOK COUNTY

Maine's largest and most northernmost county is unspoiled and unpretentious. Jutting up into the Canadian provinces of New Brunswick and

Quebec, this beautiful, rolling area is often called simply "the County" due to its vast size. Lumber barons and lumberjacks are the stuff of local legends, and towering timbers still stretch for miles in the western and northern parts. More than two thousand lakes, rivers, and streams (including the legendary Allagash Wilderness Waterway) dot the countryside, home to scores of old-fashioned fishing and hunting camps. (Some are so remote that float planes are the only way in.) The rest of the County has an almost Midwestern feel, with miles and miles of agricultural fields, most of them devoted to potatoes—a breathtaking sight when in bloom. During the fall harvest, local children are excused from school to help dig for spuds.

Picturesque and remote, Aroostook is referred to (even by Mainers) as "the other Maine." It seems almost untouched by the faster pace of life to its south. The population has declined somewhat due to lack of jobs, a condition the state's Northern Maine Development Commission is working hard to improve, but the County is as real and unspoiled as Maine gets.

Major cities in Aroostook include Presque Isle, home to about nine thousand residents, a branch of the University of Maine, a shopping mall that is popular with Canadians, and a neat old downtown. With a population of eight thousand or so, Caribou is another hub, located on the shores of the Aroostook River. Madawaska (a Maliseet Indian word meaning "land of the porcupine") is the northernmost town in Maine and a major port of Canadian

Built in 1902, Houlton's Cleveland House is a blend of Queen Anne, shingle, and colonial revival styles. It was the residence of Edward L. Cleveland, one of Aroostook County's leading potato merchants. *Photo courtesy of Maine Historic Preservation Commission.*

entry, with approximately forty-three hundred residents. Other communities in the region, most of them potato-powered, include Fort Kent (home to 3,800 and another branch of the University of Maine) and Fort Fairfield (population 3,400). Houlton is the county's oldest community and the seat of government, with close to six thousand residents. A number of its beautiful, rambling old homes and a whole section of the brick downtown are on the National Register of Historic Places.

CUMBERLAND COUNTY

The most populous county, Cumberland contains the cities of Portland, South Portland, and Westbrook, and it is the fastest-growing area in Maine.

With a population of sixty-two thousand, Portland is big enough to offer a wealth of cultural and recreational activities, yet still be of a size where folks know one another. A bustling haunt of locals and tourists alike is the Old Port, a quaint section of shops, restaurants, and offices by the waterfront, with Victorian brick buildings, wide sidewalks, and narrow cobbled streets.

Casco Bay wraps around the city, dotted by the Calendar Islands, which were named in the 1600s by Captain John Smith, who marveled, "there are as many islands as there are days in the year." (He was off slightly—there are only 136.) The city's waterfront bustles with activity. Lobstermen and fishermen off-load their catch, among the biggest in New England, and cruise ships and pleasure craft dock at Maine State Pier and Long Wharf. The *Scotia Prince*—part ferry, part cruise liner—sails daily to Nova Scotia from the International Ferry Terminal.

The major island closest to Portland is 720-acre Peaks, home to a year-round population of about fifteen hundred. Chebeague Island is the largest island in Casco Bay, supporting a year-round population of four hundred. Both have the remoteness and romance associated with islands but are within commuting distance of the city.

South Portland, one of Maine's largest cities in its own right, is home to the Portland Jetport and the Maine Mall, the state's largest retail area, full

The *Scotia Prince* can ferry two hundred cars and passengers from Portland to Nova Scotia. *Photo courtesy of Maine Office of Tourism.*

of big chain stores. Classic New England villages and wide sandy beaches surround both South Portland and Portland. The residential towns of Cape Elizabeth (more than 9,000 people), Scarborough (14,000), North Yarmouth (2,900), Falmouth (8,300), and Cumberland (6,400) are still fairly rural, but the pace of new home construction is brisk. Farther up the coast is Freeport, home of the renowned sporting goods retailer L.L. Bean as well as numerous factory outlet stores, restaurants, inns, and 7,400 residents. Brunswick, a community of more than twenty-one thousand people, has a college town feel thanks to historic Bowdoin College, but it also is the site of a major military base, the Brunswick Naval Air Station.

Inland, Sebago Lake is the second-largest in Maine and the source of much of southern Maine's drinking water. Ringed with camps, motels, and resorts, Sebago is enjoyed year-round by residents of the neighboring towns of Windham (14,000), Raymond (3,600), Naples (3,200), Bridgton (4,600), and Standish (8,400). These small towns are rapidly developing too, and are host to thousands and thousands of summer visitors.

FRANKLIN COUNTY

Franklin County rises from the central upland portion of Maine to a more mountainous region in the north. In population, Franklin is one of the state's smaller counties—about twenty-eight thousand people living in twenty-two towns and plantations. There are no cities in Franklin, and Farmington, a town of 7,883 people with a University of Maine campus, is the county's shiretown and commercial hub.

The University of Maine at Farmington was Maine's first public institution of higher education, and was recently chosen one of the top public liberal arts colleges in the nation by *U.S. News and World Report.* Known for its brick downtown and quick access to the woods, Farmington is also enjoying a quiet renaissance as a retirement center.

Beautiful and unspoiled, Franklin County is an important center for tourism. Here you'll find many outdoor recreational areas, including the Carrabassett Valley, home of Sugarloaf/USA, a popular ski mountain; Saddleback Mountain; the Bigelow mountains, and more than a hundred lakes and ponds, including those in the magnificent Rangeley Lakes region. Franklin County straddles two major watersheds, with the Dead, Carrabassett, and Sandy Rivers draining into the Kennebec River, and the Rangeley Lakes pouring westward into the Androscoggin. Rangeley Lake alone is 149 feet deep. The town of Rangeley is a nifty place, with a bustling downtown, remarkable mountain vistas, and easy access to the lakes. It's easy to understand why it was one of Maine's earliest resort areas.

Towns in Franklin County include Wilton, population about four thousand—home of the only fiddlehead canning factory in the country as well as lovely Wilson Lake—and Weld, a small community of five hundred or so, site of eight-mile-long Webb Lake and stunning Mount Blue State Park, where the peaks climb and the water is clear.

HANCOCK COUNTY

The resort town of Bar Harbor (year-round population about forty-six hundred) and extraordinarily popular Acadia National Park are the best-known features of Hancock County— between them the pair see more than three million visitors a year. Bar Harbor has all the inns, shops, and restaurants one would expect of a national-park gateway, but it's also home to a highly regarded environmental school, the College of the Atlantic.

Hancock County's Mount Desert Island (pronounced as either "desert" or "dessert") contains most of Acadia, the oldest national park east of the Mississippi River. Cadillac Mountain, the tallest peak on the eastern

Sand Beach, a popular site in Acadia National Park, as seen from the Beehive, one of the park's many hiking trails. *Photo by Nate Doudera.*

seaboard, dominates the island's eastern side. If you explore south from Ellsworth to Deer Isle, you'll find the picturesque seaside towns of Blue Hill (population 2,300), Brooklin (900), and Stonington (1,200), as well as Castine (1,300), home of Maine Maritime Academy and one of the most beautiful villages in the state.

The county is named for John Hancock, the first governor of Massachusetts, whose signature on the Declaration of Independence was three times the size of those of his compatriots. Hancock's largest city is Ellsworth, which has approximately sixty-three hundred year-round residents, a pretty old downtown, and a long stretch of strip malls. Tiny Frenchboro, on Long Island, is Hancock's smallest town, with—at last count—forty-three hardy souls.

KENNEBEC COUNTY

Maine's capital city, Augusta, straddles the banks of the river for which this county is named. Once a trading post for the Pilgrims, Augusta is today a city of twenty thousand or so, and provides a wealth of cultural and recreational activities as well as the workings of Maine's government. Nearby are the charming cities of Gardiner (6,500) and Hallowell (2,600) as well as the towns of Farmingdale (2,900) and Monmouth (3,500). The Belgrade and Winthrop Lakes Regions are popular residential and recreational areas.

In addition to the mighty Kennebec River, Kennebec County is home to scores of lakes and ponds, including the county's largest, eight-mile-long China Lake. Not far away is the city of Waterville, population sixteen thousand, and home to Colby College, one of the country's top private liberal arts institutions.

KNOX COUNTY

Established in 1860, Maine's youngest county is named for General Henry Knox, George Washington's Secretary of War during the American Revolution. A replica of General Knox's mansion, Montpelier, stands in the coastal town of Thomaston (population about 3,313). The largest city is Rockland, an eclectic mix of working waterfront and artsy downtown, which is currently enjoying great prosperity thanks to the Farnsworth Art Museum, one of the nation's best small museums. Rockland is home to about eight thousand people. In recent years this part of Maine's midcoast region has experienced rapid growth due to the major expansion of the credit card bank MBNA.

Several towns in Knox County, including Rockland, Rockport (population three thousand), and Owls Head, flank Penobscot Bay, world renowned for its fine sailing. The Camden Hills, a ridge of low mountains that stretch along the coast, offer sweeping views of Penobscot bay and its two-hundred-odd islands. Snuggled between the mountains and the sea is the town of Camden, a vacation hotspot.

Knox County is a mix of bustling tourist towns, quiet fishing villages, rural inland communities, and hundreds of islands—some of them inhabited year-round. North Haven and Vinalhaven, known together as the Fox Islands, are both serviced by ferries from Rockland. A genuine working island, Vinalhaven has approximately thirteen-hundred residents, while the more genteel North Haven has about three hundred. Matinicus, about twenty miles offshore from Rockland, is Maine's most remote inhabited island, with a year-round population of about seventy-five.

LINCOLN COUNTY

Most people think this county is named for our country's sixteenth president, but actually it is a tribute to Thomas Pownal, a Massachu-setts governor whose home was Lincoln, Eng-land. Lincoln County is home to approximately thirty thousand Mainers and is a mix of coastal and inland towns and offshore islands such as the artist colony of Monhegan.

Lincoln County contains no cities, and the area's largest town is Waldoboro, with a population of about five thousand. Waldoboro was settled around 1740 by German families who were brought to America by General Samuel Waldo. Wiscasset (accent on the second syl-lable) is the next largest community, with about three thousand residents. This town bills itself as "the prettiest village in Maine," and it is indeed a charming place of fine architecture, nestled alongside the Sheepscot River. Other communities in Lincoln County include Boothbay (population 2,800), well-known resort Boothbay Harbor (2,300), and Newcastle (1,700). Dam-ariscotta (1,800), located between the ocean and lovely Damariscotta Lake, is a bustling place during the warmer months and has seen an influx of re-tirees in recent years.

Monhegan, reached by ferry from Port Clyde, is probably Maine's most famous island, thanks to the work of such internationally known artists as Rockwell Kent, Edward Hopper, and Jamie Wyeth. Located about ten miles out to sea, Monhegan is less than a mile wide and about two miles long, yet seventeen miles of trails wind around its nature preserves and spectacular cliffs, including the legendary Cathedral Woods. The island has a year-round population of about seventy-five and no automobile traffic.

OXFORD COUNTY

Oxford sits smack in the middle of Maine's western mountains, and part of the White Mountains National Forest is located in this region, as are lovely lakes, ski areas, and resorts that draw tourists year-round. Bethel, called the classic New England village by many, is nestled in the Oxford Hills along the Androscoggin River. About twenty-five hundred people live in Bethel's pretty old homes and farms. Close by is the Sunday River Ski Resort and the Sunday River Bridge, one of the most photographed covered bridges in the state. The foreign-sounding Maine towns of Norway (4,900), Mexico (3,300), Denmark (900), Sweden (240), and Paris (4,600) are all located in Oxford County.

Rumford, with a population of nearly seven thousand, is the largest community in Oxford County and the home of Mead Publishing Paper Division, a massive paper mill. Rumford has a ninety-seven-bed community hospital, as well as the small Black Mountain Ski Area. Rumford and nearby Mexico are part of the scenic River Valley, so named because it is where the Androscoggin and Swift Rivers converge.

PENOBSCOT COUNTY

Penobscot County was named for the mighty river that meanders through the region. One of Maine's prime whitewater rafting areas is on the river's west branch. Also situated along the river is one of the state's largest cities—Bangor.

Once known only for its colorful history as a logging town (a thirty-one-foot statue of Paul Bunyan welcomes visitors), Bangor today is a city of thirty-one thousand residents and boasts a lively arts scene, state-of-the-art health-care facilities (including Eastern Maine Medical Center), and a growing importance in foreign trade and travel thanks to Bangor International Airport. It is home to the Bangor Auditorium—a six-thousand-seat hall hosting everything from concerts to garden shows—as well as the Bangor Civic Center and the Bangor Fairgrounds.

Bordering Bangor is Orono, population ninety-two hundred, home to the main campus of the University of Maine. The University is a city within itself, comprising more than eight thousand acres and 158 buildings, and featuring the Maine Center for the Arts, a concert hall that brings many national acts to the area.

The working city of Brewer (8,684 inhabitants) and the charming riverside town of Hampden (6,200) are nearby communities, as is the city of Old Town (8,000), famous for its finely crafted Old Town Canoes. Millinocket (population 6,600) is located about seventy miles up the Penobscot from Bangor at the northern end of the county. Known for its huge paper mill, it's also the gateway to the extraordinary wilderness area called Baxter State Park.

PISCATAQUIS COUNTY

Piscataquis County takes its name from the Abnaki term meaning "at the river branch," and it is Maine's third-largest county. Within its boundaries are two-hundred-thousand-acre Baxter State Park as well as Maine's highest mountain, Mount Katahdin. Baxter was a gift to the people of Maine by Governor Percival Baxter, who stipulated that the park be kept forever wild. Excellent fishing, mountain climbing, and hiking are found on its 175 miles of trails. Piscataquis County also contains much of the Allagash Wilderness Waterway, a nationally known canoe route.

Heavily forested, with a low population density, Piscataquis has about eighteen thousand residents. The town of Dover-Foxcroft, with 4,272 people, is the largest community and a business center for the surrounding area. A pretty town of graceful old homes, it is situated on the Piscataquis River. Greenville, population eighteen hundred, is on the banks of seventy-five thousand-acre Moosehead Lake, the biggest lake contained in one state this side of the Mississippi. The town is a wilderness outpost, known for moose and four-season outdoor recreation. A spectacular site at Moosehead is majestic Mt. Kineo, which rises out of the water forming a sheer seven-hundred-foot cliff.

SAGADAHOC COUNTY

With only 257 square miles, this is Maine's smallest county. Bath, located along the Kennebec River, is Sagadahoc's largest city, with a population of ten thousand. Bath has been a shipbuilding center since the eighteenth century, and the tradition continues today at Bath Iron Works, where massive ships are constructed for the navy. Bath boasts handsome homes and a brick downtown as well as the Maine Maritime Museum.

Topsham, with about nine thousand residents, is the next-largest community, as well as the area's fastest-growing town. The towns of Bowdoin (2,700) and Bowdoinham (2,500) are bucolic villages near massive Merrymeeting Bay, where five large rivers meet and where migrating ducks and geese rest en route to warmer climes. Woolwich (2,800) is a rural town located across the Kennebec from Bath.

SOMERSET COUNTY

The land area of Somerset county—3,903 square miles—makes it Maine's second-largest. Extending from the Canadian border all the way to Fairfield in central Maine, the area is almost 90 percent forested, and borders Moosehead Lake and the Allagash Wilderness Waterway. Flagstaff Lake, as well as much of the Dead River, a popular rafting spot, are located in Somerset County.

Skowhegan is the largest community, with a population of 9,790. The home of the late Margaret Chase Smith, the first woman to serve in both the U.S. House and Senate, Skowhegan is also the site of one of Maine's largest agricultural fairs and a prestigious school of painting. Fairfield (6,700), Pittsfield (4,100), and Madison (4,600) are other sizable towns in Somerset County. The Forks and Caratunk, tiny villages both, are at the epicenter of Maine's whitewater rafting industry.

WALDO COUNTY

Belfast (population about sixty-five hundred) is the largest community in Waldo county, and the area's only city. Once known more for its chicken processing plants than its lovely harbor, Belfast today is a mix of lively downtown shops, businesses, and elegant homes from the 1800s. Deemed "culturally cool" in *USA Today,* the city is home to a number of artists, has a theater troupe, a huge co-op, a dance studio, and a movie theater that plays art films.

Waldo County's coastal towns include Lincolnville (2,000) and Searsport (2,700), famous for its sea captain's homes. Several of its small inland communities bear patriotic names: Liberty (804), Freedom (699) and Unity (about 2,000). Waldo county has grown in recent years, thanks to the expansion of credit-card giant MBNA and smaller local heroes such as Moss, Inc. There is a small but excellent hospital—Waldo County General, in Belfast. Islesboro (population 600) is home to a tony island community where actor John Travolta has a summer place.

WASHINGTON COUNTY

The easternmost county in the nation, Washington is nicknamed "The Sunrise County" because many argue that the sun hits here first as it wakes up the United States. A trip through this part of Maine reveals rocky and sandy beaches, dramatic oceanside cliffs, the highest tides in the country, and acres and acres of windswept blueberry barrens, home to Maine's thriving lowbush blueberry industry. Nature preserves dot the landscape: Petit Manan in Steuben, Great Wass Island in Jonesport-Beals, Roque Bluffs State Park in Machias, Cobscook Bay State Park in Dennysville, and Moosehorn National Wildlife Refuge in Calais— all set before miles and miles of oceanfront.

This is the quietest coastal region in Maine, a place where tradition still reigns and where tourism is welcome but not counted upon. Fishing and blueberrying are the major industries. The primary city is Calais (pronounced CAL-us), which has about four thousand residents and is connected by a bridge to St. Stephen, New Brunswick. Eastport (population about two thousand) is the easternmost city in United States, and it has a lovely and historic brick downtown. Because of its situation on Moose Island, just about every house in Eastport has a fantastic view of Passamaquoddy Bay. Other important towns in the county are Lubec (2,000) and Machias (2,500), home to a branch of the University of Maine.

YORK COUNTY

Maine's oldest and most southerly county was created in 1652 as Yorkshire Province. This stretch of Maine is famous for its broad white beaches and picturesque New England towns. York's coast is the home of the famed villages of Kennebunkport (population 3,500) and Ogunquit (1,000), where tourists flock by the thousands in the summer. From Kittery (9,200) in the south, known for its outlet shopping, to Old Orchard Beach (7,700) in the north, a beachfront boardwalk community famous for its honky-tonk atmosphere, the southern Maine coast is popular both with vacationers and new Mainers, many of whom commute to Portland or Portsmouth, New Hampshire, for jobs. Some of Maine's wealthiest communities are in York County, as well as many of the fastest-growing towns.

The neighboring cities of Biddeford and Saco (with populations of 20,000 and 15,000 respectively) together make up York County's largest center of commerce. The towns of Sanford (20,000) and Wells (8,100) are other notable spots.

Politics

STATE GOVERNMENT

Like many states, Maine has three governing branches: executive, legislative, and judiciary. The head of the executive branch is the governor, elected to a term of four years. The governor can serve no more than two

MAINE'S FASTEST GROWING AREAS

Here are a dozen areas with the highest gains in population according to a 1999 report of the Maine State Housing Authority.

Belfast Area (Belfast, Belmont, Brooks, Frankfort, Islesboro, Jackson, Knox, Liberty, Lincolnville, Monroe, Montville, Morrill, Northport, Searsmont, Searsport, Swanville, Waldo, Dixmont)
Population: +1.3%   Housing: +1.8%   Jobs: +7.3%

Outer Bangor Area (Bradford, Carmel, Charleston, Corinth, Hudson, Levant, Newburgh, Alton, Greenbush, Greenfield, LaGrange)
Population: +1.1%   Housing: +1.6%   Jobs: +1.1%

Bucksport Area (Bucksport, Dedham, Orland, Verona, Prospect, Stockton Springs)
Population: +1.0%   Housing: +1.2%   Jobs: +.5%

Sanford Area (Acton, Alfred, Lebanon, Limerick, Newfield, North Berwick, Sanford, Shapleigh, Waterboro)
Population: +.8%   Housing: +.90%   Jobs: +2.7%

Kittery–York Area (Berwick, Eliot, Kittery, South Berwick, York)
Population: +.8%   Housing: +1.10%   Jobs: –2.7%

Sebago Lake Area (Baldwin, Bridgton, Naples, Sebago, Denmark, Fryeburg, Hiram, Brownfield, Porter, Cornish, Parsonsfield, Lovell, Harrison, Stoneham, Stow, Sweden, Waterford)
Population: +.8%   Housing: 1.1%   Jobs: 3.6%

Ellsworth–Bar Harbor Area (Amherst, Aurora, Bar Harbor, Cranberry Isles, Eastbrook, Ellsworth, Franklin, Gouldsboro, Hancock, Lamoine, Mariaville, Mount Desert, Otis, Sorrento, Southwest Harbor, Sullivan, Surry, Tremont, Trenton, Waltham, Winter Harbor, Bradley, Clifton, Steuben)
Population: +.8%   Housing: +1.1%   Jobs: +4.1%

Norway-Paris Area (Minot, Otisfield, Buckfield, Hebron, Norway, Oxford, Paris, Sumner, West Paris)
Population: +.7%   Housing: +1.0%   Jobs: +2.8%

consecutive terms, and the state does not have a lieutenant governor. If the governor dies or becomes unable to govern, the succession passes to the president of the senate and next to the speaker of the house.

The Maine legislature is composed of the house of representatives and the senate. The Maine House of Representatives consists of 151 members (one of the largest in the country) plus two nonvoting members representing the Penobscot Nation and the Passamaquoddy Tribe. Each house member represents a district of approximately 8,132 people.

The Maine Senate is the upper chamber and serves as the final confirming body of all bills passed before they are sent to the governor. There are thirty-five senators, and at this writing, nineteen are Maine natives and sixteen are women. Maine ranks second in the nation for the percentage of women elected to the senate (45 percent—Washington state has 46.9 per-

Biddeford Area (Arundel, Biddeford, Dayton, Kennebunk, Kennebunkport, Lyman, Saco, Ogunquit, Wells)
Population: +.7%   Housing: +.07%   Jobs: +2.5%

Bath–Brunswick Area (Durham, Brunswick, Harpswell, New Gloucester, Pownal, Dresden, Arrowsic, Bath, Bowdoin, Bowdoinham, Georgetown, Phippsburg, Topsham, West Bath, Woolwich, Richmond, Alna, Edgecomb, Wiscasset, Westport Island)
Population: +.6%   Housing: +1.2%   Jobs: –0.2 %

Greater Portland Area (Cape Elizabeth, Casco, Cumberland, Falmouth, Freeport, Gorham, Gray, North Yarmouth, Long Island, Portland, Raymond, Scarborough, South Portland, Standish, Westbrook, Windham, Yarmouth, Buxton, Hollis, Limington, Old Orchard Beach)
Population: +.5%   Housing: +1.0%   Jobs: +3.3%

Rockland Area (Appleton, Camden, Cushing, Friendship, Hope, Matinicus, North Haven, Owl's Head, Rockland, Rockport, St. George, South Thomaston, Thomaston, Union, Vinalhaven, Warren, Washington, Criehaven, Waldoboro)
Population: +.5%   Housing: +.8%   Jobs: +2.3 %

Maine's capitol building was constructed in 1910.
Photo courtesy of Maine Office of Tourism.

cent) and is the only state to have three women holding senate leadership positions during the same session.

Elected to two-year terms, the legislators pass the laws, confirm judges, and choose four constitutional officers, who also serve two-year terms: attorney general, secretary of state, state treasurer, state auditor. The effect of this procedure is to allow the majority party to control the constitutional offices.

Maine is one of three states with a joint standing budget committee system. The state budget must receive a two-thirds vote of the legislature, and the governor does not possess line-item veto power.

The judicial branch is headed by the Supreme Judicial Court, with a chief justice and six associate justices to handle appeals from lower courts. Criminal and court cases requiring a trial by jury are heard by the Superior Court, while civil actions, traffic infractions, juvenile cases, and small claims are heard in Maine's thirty-three district courts. Each county has a probate court to handle wills, estates, adoptions, and appointment of guardians. Probate in Maine, unlike in other states, is considered a simple, prompt, and relatively inexpensive process.

LOCAL GOVERNMENT

Government in Maine, as in much of New England, has a strong local bias, with the town unit at its foundation. Towns (currently there are 424) must be incorporated, requiring a legislative act but not a charter. Towns are governed by the quintessential example of direct democracy—the annual town meeting and elected officials called selectmen. Since 1970, towns in Maine have operated under home rule, which means they may make many of their own decisions without going before the state legislature.

Maine's cities, numbering twenty-two, must be chartered by the legislature. All have a representative form of government called the city council.

Population size doesn't always indicate city or town status. Eastport, in Washington County, for example, is a city of about two thousand citizens, while Brunswick, with a population of more than twenty thousand, is a town.

In addition to cities and towns, Maine still has examples of plantations, an archaic form of local government used centuries ago in Massachusetts. Plantations are mini-towns, usually populated by fewer than one hundred people, incorporated by the commissioners of the county in which they are located. Although Maine's fifty-one plantations have fewer rights than do towns and do not operate under home rule, they are governed in much the same way, with an annual meeting and elected officials called assessors. Monhegan Island is probably the best known of Maine's plantations.

In addition to plantations, Maine has another unique twist: 416 unorganized townships. Almost half the state's land area falls in this category. These very sparsely populated townships have no local government. They are supervised and taxed directly by the state. Some have regular names—Attean Township, Chain of Ponds Township—but many are identified only by their location in a surveyor's grid: T5 R17 or T3 R12, for example.

PROFILE

Jay Culberth and Lynn Johnson moved to Maine from Minnesota and Ohio, respectively. They lived in Portland for a few years before moving to Poland in 1998. "We wanted to live on a mountain or lake, and our real-estate agent found us a place on a lovely little pond," Lynn explains. "The house is a fishing shack from 1940, and it sits on a peninsula. We love watching the water and the wildlife."

Jay works for the American Skiing Company in Bethel and is also a member of Poland's planning board. Lynn is employed by Idexx Corp., a biotechnology firm in Westbrook. Androscoggin County has worked out well for their respective commutes. "Poland is real small-town living," says Lynn. "It's one of those towns where, if you blink, you've missed it. We appreciate the quiet and the friendly townspeople and neighbors. We absolutely love living here."

Maine's sixteen counties are governed by commissioners who are elected by the people. County budgets are determined by the legislature. In some states, county government is very powerful, but this isn't really true in Maine. Counties are primarily responsible for running jails and sheriffs' departments, and county offices house registries of probate and deeds.

POLITICAL PARTIES

The independent Maine spirit is especially apparent at the voting booth, where people tend to vote their conscience rather than their party affiliation. In the past twenty-five years, Maine has had two independent governors: James Longley, elected in 1974, and Angus S. King, Jr., elected to a first term in 1994 and reelected in 1998 by one of the largest margins in Maine's history.

The newest political development is the legitimization of two additional political parties. Thanks to a recent state law, The Green Independent and Reform parties are now listed on state income tax forms for donations, as well as on voter registration applications. These parties may also join with Maine Democrats and Republicans in presidential primaries and other elections.

Taxes

"Maine's low tax base means a high tax burden," observes Gary Swanson, who moved here with his family from Oakland, California, in 1998. Another former Californian agrees. "We moved here believing that the cost of living would be substantially lower," says Brad Rourke, of Camden. "It isn't."

PROPERTY TAX

With regard to state and local taxes, it sometimes seems as if Mainers shoulder a heavy load. Residents of Maine bear the thirteenth-highest state and local tax burden in the country, largely due to high property taxes, the lion's share of which goes to pay for public schools. The U.S. Commerce Department reports that, in relative terms, Mainers pay the fourth-heaviest property levy in the country, averaging fifty-two dollars in property tax for evey one thousand dollars earned.

In an effort to soften the tax blow, Maine has trimmed its sales tax (in July 2000 the rate dropped from 5.5 percent to 5 percent), increased personal exemptions on the state income tax, and offered property tax breaks to homeowners. A new program that reimburses businesses for property taxes on new equipment saved Mainers about $42 million in 1998. Tax reformers believe more relief is in sight.

But tax bites depend on many factors, including income brackets and which taxes are considered. A recent Citizens for Tax Justice analysis suggests that for middle income Maine people, state and local taxes are actually the same or lower than the national average. Their analysis places greater weight on Maine's progressive income tax structure, which requires wealthy people to pay more here than in other states.

One reason for high local taxes is that traditionally Mainers have balked at consolidation of services on the county model, preferring instead a type of government that is close to the people. However, this means that individual towns are expected to provide a high level of services, including police and fire protection, road maintenance, and public assistance.

Tax burdens are relative. Retirees Bill and Allie Lou Richardson, of Islesboro, find Maine's taxes significantly lower than what they paid in New York. New Rockport resident Lynda Chilton says, "We have a lower cost of living here than in Virginia and better services. Really, to me, Maine defines the phrase 'quality of life.'"

Here's how some of Maine's state taxes break down. For more information, call the Maine Revenue Service at 207-626-8475, or try its website at http://janus.state.me.us/revenue/.

INDIVIDUAL INCOME TAX

Maine has a graduated individual income tax rate, similar to the federal tax structure. Tax rates are 2 percent, 4.5 percent, 7 percent, and 8.5 percent. The applicable rate depends on marginal income. For example, a single taxpayer with $20,000 of taxable income would pay 2 percent on the first $4,150; 4.5 percent on the on the next $4,100, 7 percent on the following $8,250, and 8.5 percent on the final $3,500 of taxable income.

For 1999 the personal exemption amount was $2,750; and standard deduction amounts began at $4,300 for single filers and $7,200 for married joint filers. An additional amount of $1,050 is allowed for taxpayers over age sixty-five.

Income tax revenues go into the state's general fund.

Highest Individual Income Tax Rates

North Dakota	12.0	New York	7.125
Hawaii	10.0	New Jersey	6.37
Iowa	8.98	Massachusetts	5.95
Maine	8.5	Connecticut	4.5
Minnesota	8.5		

CORPORATE INCOME TAX

Maine also has a graduated rate for corporate income tax. Tax rates are 3.5 percent for the first $25,000 of Maine net income; 7.93 percent for the next $50,000; 8.33 percent for the following $175,000, and 8.93 percent for Maine net incomes in excess of $250,000. A number of tax-credit programs have been established to spur investment, including the High Technology Credit, the Research and Development Expense Super Credit, and the Maine Seed Capital/Venture Capital Tax Credits.

REAL ESTATE TRANSFER TAX

A real-estate transfer tax is imposed on both the seller and buyer at the rate of $1.10 per $500 of property, including the value of any mortgage or other encumbrance. Half of the money raised benefits the state's general fund, the rest goes to the county in which the sale occurred.

ESTATE TAX

The estate of any Maine resident, or of any nonresident with real and tangible property located in Maine, is *possibly* subject to Maine estate tax. The tax is in the amount of the federal credit for state death taxes and is due nine months after the date of death.

MOTOR VEHICLE EXCISE TAX

"The tax on our cars was an unpleasant surprise," recalls Jan Njaa, who moved to Belfast from Chicago in June 1999.

Maine's motor vehicle excise tax is based on the manufacturer's list price of a vehicle including all options, at a rate ranging from 24 mills ($24 per $1,000 in value) for new vehicles down to 4 mills ($4 per $1,000) for older models. The tax base is the purchase price in the original year of title, applying to motor vehicles, aircraft, camper trailers, truck campers, and mobile homes used on public roads. It's paid to the municipality every year at registration time.

GASOLINE EXCISE TAX

Mainers pay a tax of twenty-two cents a gallon on gasoline and twenty-three cents a gallon on diesel fuel. Monies raised go to the highway and general funds.

SALES TAX

The general sales tax was reduced to 5 percent from 5.5 percent in July 2000. Grocery food items are not taxed, except for items defined as snack foods. The rate is higher for restaurant meals and lodging (7 percent) and car rentals (10 percent).

Spending and Saving

MAINE STATE LOTTERY

The first state-approved lottery conducted in Maine was back in 1823, when permission was granted to raise $50,000 for a canal-building corporation in southern Maine. The Maine State Lottery was created in 1973, with the first games conducted June 27, 1974. Profits go to the general fund.

Maine is a partner (with New Hampshire and Vermont) in the Tri-State Lottery Commission. The most popular lotto game is the Tri-State Megabucks, drawn on Wednesday and Saturday. The top megabucks jackpot so far was $16.4 million in January 1992.

Other lotto games include 5 Card Cash, drawn on Tuesday and Friday, and WinCash, a rolling jackpot game with prizes paid out in a one-time cash payment. There are also Pick 3 and Pick 4 games.

Maine also promotes two dozen or so instant scratch games, including the Maine Outdoor Heritage Game. Profits from this ticket are earmarked for a fund to conserve wildlife and open spaces, with grants totaling approximately $1.5 million awarded annually.

If you hold a winning ticket in one of Maine's games, you have 180 days from the date your prize is won to claim your new fortune. (Maine State Lottery Commission phone number: 287-3721.)

RECYCLING

While recycling may be a fairly novel concept in many states, it is nothing new in Maine. Frugal Yankees that they are, Mainers have been recycling in one form or another for generations. Second-hand shops, swap shops, and yard sales are popular, not because Mainers don't like to buy new things but because they like a bargain. It is not surprising that Amy Dacyczyn, the author of the popular *Tightwad Gazette* newsletter of the 1990s, lives thriftily in Leeds, Maine. There is a real aversion to the disposable culture in the Pine Tree State. As the old-timers still say, "Use it up, wear it out, make it do, or do without."

Recycling household trash and composting organic waste is the focus of the Maine State Planning Office's Waste Management and Recycling Program. Communities are not required by law to have recycling programs in place, but nearly all of them do. For one thing, it saves money; most communities have to pay dearly to truck their solid waste to one of the few waste incinerators or approved landfill sites. In most of Maine the soils are not suitable for landfills.

Each community develops its own recycling program, selects the materials it wishes to include, and determines its own collection methods and markets. This hands-off approach has worked: Maine has among the highest recycling rates in the nation and has become a national model for both environmental sensitivity and economic sensibility.

THE BOTTLE BILL

The state was also one of the first to enact a bottle bill for beer and soda. The bill was passed in the late seventies as an attempt to curb roadside litter, but today the effort is viewed in the larger context of recycling, and includes more types of beverages, such as bottled water and fruit drinks. Small bottles or cans (four liters or less) require a nickel deposit; larger bottles such as wine or liquor require fifteen cents. Bottles may be redeemed at many grocery stores, supermarkets, and at redemption centers around the state. Aseptic packaging (juice boxes) as well as certain beverages (milk and hand-pressed cider) are exempt from the regulations.

3 Working in Maine

"As a former business owner, I often consider myself an executive on loan to Maine. My number one priority is creating an environment in which businesses can thrive."

—GOVERNOR ANGUS S. KING, JR.*

It seems you can't talk about Maine's economy today without mentioning the boom and bust decade of the 1980s, which affected all of New England. During that turbulent time, the economy grew by leaps and bounds, only to bust like an old potato basket in 1990, throwing the state into a deep recession. The years that followed were devastating for many Mainers. From 1989 to 1992, thirty thousand jobs were lost, many of them in the manufacturing industry, once a mainstay of the state's economy. Young working-age residents, particularly in central and northern Maine, began leaving in droves to search for jobs elsewhere.

Fortunately, the recession slowly ended, and for many, 1997 marked the year the state could claim a full recovery. The climb back was gradual, but steady—a moderate kind of growth experts say is far preferable to the heady days of the eighties. Under the leadership of Governor Angus King, the state mounted an aggressive economic development strategy aimed at creating new jobs, cutting workers' compensation insurance costs, lowering electric utility rates, reforming taxes, and building a state-of-the-art telecommunications infrastructure. The impact of these efforts on Maine's business climate has been dramatic.

----

*Quoted in the *Portland Press Herald*.

A Growing Economy

Today the Maine economy is expanding. The past few years have seen steady job growth (sixty-five thousand new jobs since 1995) as thriving businesses take on more workers. New companies have come in, creating opportunities in brand new sectors like telemarketing and biotechnology. From 1999 to mid-2000 the unemployment rate has ranged between 3.3 percent (an all-time low) and 4.2 percent, as evidenced by many help wanted signs displayed in the windows of shops and offices. Other indicators of a growing economy, such as retail sales, construction contract awards, and building permits, have all risen significantly. And since 1993, the number of Maine people receiving welfare is down by 45 percent.

Although a disproportionate number of new jobs are in southern Maine, the state is working hard to spread the wealth and create opportunities in more remote areas. An initiative of the Maine Department of Economic and Community Development called "One Maine" is trying to attract businesses to those areas that have lagged behind in the state's recovery. The efforts are starting to pay off. For instance, a telecommunications company has recently opened in Calais, providing employment for 150 Washington County residents.

Why Do Business in Maine?

Maine in the new millennium offers many advantages to businesses, starting with Mainers themselves. Maine's people are dependable, hardworking, and willing to master new skills. Next, consider the state's telecommunications network, which is considered by many to be the best in the nation, with more than eighty thousand miles of fiber optics, the country's first digitally switched communications network, and more band width all the time. The state's location is a boon for international trade, not only because it is coastal, making for easy shipping, but it also borders Canada, an important trading partner. Finally, the state's transportation infrastructure (roads, airports, freight lines, and ports) offers uncrowded, high-quality avenues to quickly move products. Add to these benefits Maine's business climate, which fosters risk-taking and entrepreneurial efforts, and the result is a winning economic situation.

A MAINE SUCCESS STORY

The world's leader in the outdoor-specialty field, L.L. Bean, is headquartered in Freeport in a 109,000 square-foot Main Street store and the adjacent 17,000 square-foot L.L. Kids store. To glance around at the more than sixteen thousand items in the main store alone, amongst the more than 3.5 million customers who flock there each year, you'd be hard pressed to believe it all started with one humble shoe and one entrepreneurial Mainer.

The company was founded in 1912 by Leon Leonwood Bean, who developed the gum-soled Maine Hunting Shoe to avoid soggy feet when traipsing through the woods. Initially, his product was manufactured in one room and sold exclusively through catalogs to other hunting enthusiasts. Today, "Bean's" sells to 147 countries around the world, with annual sales totaling more than $1 billion, produces approximately fifty different catalogs each year, and has nine locations in the United States and more than a dozen retail stores in Japan. L.L. Bean employs more than ten thousand workers during the peak holiday season and is Maine's third-largest employer.

The original L.L. Bean retail store as it looked in the 1930s.
Photo courtesy of L.L. Bean, Inc.

Traditional Maine Employment

In a 1998 report, *Issues Facing the Maine Economy,* State Economist Laurie Lachance noted that Maine's economic vitality has "long been based on the bounty of our natural resources—fishing, farming, forestry, and tourism. The very nature of these industries has meant that a significant portion of our employment opportunities are seasonal and overall earnings lag behind national averages." The changing composition of Maine's job base has also posed challenges. "Fifty years ago, one out of every two jobs in Maine was in the manufacturing sector," wrote Lachance. "That figure has now fallen to around 15 percent."

Other factors have strongly influenced the Pine Tree State's economy in recent years. Globalization of the marketplace, development of new technologies, and an aging population have all had significant impacts on working people, many of whom—unlike fifty years ago—are women. But rather than confounding Mainers, these challenges have spurred them to use the Yankee ingenuity and solid work ethic for which they're famous to adapt and thrive in the face of change.

Although horses have been replaced by machines, logging is a traditional occupation that remains vital to Maine's economy. *Photo courtesy Maine State Museum.*

The credit card bank MBNA has offices in Brunswick, Camden, Orono, Portland, Presque Isle, Fort Kent, Farmington, and Rockland, with operational headquarters located in this building in Belfast. Two thousand people work in the Belfast facility alone. *Photo courtesy MBNA New England.*

The New Maine Economy

Are good-paying jobs available? What kinds of businesses does the state attract? These are a few of the questions prospective new residents consider when beginning a job search in Maine. "Jason and I wondered if we would find lucrative jobs that offered rewarding work," says Kristine Scher of Rockland. "We did—Jason has a good position with MBNA, and I'm enjoying a challenging job at Northeast Health."

The Schers found employment in two of Maine's fastest-growing business sectors: call centers and health care. Telemarketing centers, such as those of MBNA New England, the credit card giant, or of EnvisionNet, a Brunswick-based computer support outfit, are replacing scores of jobs lost during the recession of the early nineties. For many Maine residents, these new areas of employment offer training in customer service and computer skills as well as valuable experience that may open up other opportunities for future work.

Telecommunications

It may not mesh with the state's moose-and-mountains image, but Maine boasts a new high-tech telephone system that is, according to the president of Bell Atlantic, "the best in the United States, if not the world." Completion of the fiber-optic system in autumn of 1999 linked Aroostook County with an existing system of lines in other parts of the state, assuring that phone connections across Maine are top of the line.

The eighty thousand or so miles of fiber-optic cable in Maine's system mean more than just clear conversations with Aunt Elsie. The system is capable of carrying millions of voice, data, and video signals daily and includes 100 percent digital phone switching technology as well as self-healing technologies in the event something goes awry. In short, the $100-million investment puts Maine solidly in the forefront as a telecommunications leader.

According to a March 2000 report from the Federal Communications Commission, Maine ranks second in the nation in the percentage of households with telephone service. An estimated 97.6% of Maine households have phones, well above the national average of 94%. (Delaware ranks first with 98.2%.) Twenty-four phone companies keep connections clear and crisp, with Bell Atlantic—serving 85% of the state—the largest. Local companies, although small in comparison, are no lightweights when it comes to telecommunications. "All of Maine's phone companies, including the twenty-three independent local companies, are tied in to the inter- and intrastate fiber optic network," says Phil Lindley of the Public Utilities Commission. "Regardless of size, they have state-of-the art technology, and in many cases, can connect people to the Internet with a local phone call." Smaller phone companies, says Lindley, are linked to the folks they serve in more ways than one. "Local phone companies tend to be community-minded," he notes. "And since they truly know their customers, they offer exceptional customer service."

Maine is already home to a number of businesses that rely on this sophisticated and reliable telecommunications infrastructure for their call centers and communication networks. L.L. Bean, Talk America, MBNA New England, EnvisionNet, and Auto Europe all maintain large and complex call centers that serve a global customer base. According to the Maine Department of Economic and Community Development, L.L. Bean alone

LARGEST EMPLOYERS IN MAINE (AS OF 3/99)

Compiled by the Center for Business and Economic Research, University of Southern Maine

Company	Employees	Type of Business
1. Bath Iron Works	7400–7600	Shipbuilding
2. Hannaford Brothers	6800–7000	Grocer
3. L.L. Bean, Inc.	5400–5600	Retail
4. Wal-Mart Associates, Inc.	4200–4400	Retail
5. Maine Medical Ctr.	4000–4200	Health services
6. UnumProvident Life Insurance Co.	3600–3800	Insurance
7. Shaws Supermarkets, Inc.	3200–3400	Grocer
8. Eastern Maine Medical Ctr.	2400–2600	Health services
9. MBNA Marketing Systems	2400–2600	Credit cards
10. Maine General Medical Ctr.	2000–2200	Health services
11. Central Maine Power Co.	1600–1800	Utility
12. Great Northern Paper, Inc.	1600–1800	Paper manufacturer
13. Pratt & Whitney Group	1600–1800	Aircraft parts
14. S.D. Warren	1600–1800	Paper manufacturer
15. Irving Oil Corporation	1400–1600	Gasoline service stations
16. Maine Blue Cross & Blue Shield	1400–1600	Insurance
17. New England Telephone	1400–1600	Telecommunications
18. Rite-Aid of Maine, Inc.	1400–1600	Pharmacy
19. Ames Department Stores	1200–1400	Retail
20. Central Maine Medical Ctr.	1200–1400	Health services
21. Champion International Corp.	1200–1400	Paper manufacturer
22. International Paper Co.	1200–1400	Paper manufacturer
23. Mead Oxford Corp.	1200–1400	Paper manufacturer
24. Sunday River Skiway Corp.	1200–1400	Recreation
25. Dexter Shoe Co.	1000–1200	Shoe manufacturer
26. Fairchild Semiconductor	1000–1200	Electronics manufacturer
27. Fraser Paper Ltd.	1000–1200	Paper manufacturer
28. Manpower	1000–1200	Temporary agency
29. Mercy Hospital	1000–1200	Health services
30. Peoples Heritage Savings Bank	1000–1200	Savings institution
31. Attendant Services, Inc.	800–1000	Social services
32. Bates College	800–1000	College
33. Blethen Maine Newspapers	800–1000	Publisher
34. Bowdoin College	800–1000	College
35. Brown Company	800–1000	Gasoline service stations

received 14-million toll-free catalog and customer service calls in 1996. The statewide availability of cutting-edge fiber-optic technology means businesses are free to expand or set up shop anywhere in the state.

Health Care

Health care is an increasingly important force in the economy as well. According to the Maine Hospital Association, health care directly accounts for sixty thousand full- and part-time jobs and up to thirty-five thousand related jobs. Indeed, the health care industry is responsible for roughly 10 percent of all jobs in the state and 15 percent of the private sector's payroll.

Through a well-designed website (http://www.themrc.com/) as well as more traditional methods, the Maine Hospital Association's Recruitment Center actively courts health care providers, especially physicians. The center offers the latest information about health care opportunities and provides confidential job searches, all with the aim of attracting top-notch professionals to high-tech hospitals in Maine's pristine, low-key setting. Many physicians find the lure irresistible.

Howard Jones practices internal and occupational medicine in the mid-coast: "I went online during the summer of 1998 and made a connection with Waldo County General Hospital in Belfast. They invited me up, and when I arrived it was a beautiful August day. Everything looked like the cover of a *Down East* magazine. I liked both the hospital and the people I met. That winter, my family and I left North Carolina for Maine.

"Those of us in the medical field are fortunate, because we can live just about anywhere and make a decent living," Jones continues. "Practicing medicine in Maine is really nice. You have a different kind of relationship with patients than in other places, because you'll actually see them again in the community. There's a wide cross-section of people, and not very many managed-care companies to put a wall between you and your patients. And I think the people in Maine are hardy, healthy souls."

Biotechnology

Maine's emerging biotechnology industry is one of the fastest-growing sectors of the economy, offering more than 650 different products and services to national and international markets. According to the Biotechnology Association of Maine, a trade association representing the growing community of biotech companies, more than forty-seven hundred Mainers are employed by biotech companies, nonprofit and government laboratories, and educational institutions throughout the state. Industries as diverse as aquaculture, diagnostics, immunodiagnostics, marine science, microbiology, and pharmacology are part of this new force in the Maine economy, and its steady growth has been a focus of the state's economic planners.

Natural Resources

Magnificent natural resources have long been the backbone of the state's economy. Fishing, hunting, rafting, skiing, snowmobiling, and forest-based manufacturing industries are all dependent on Maine's woods, waters, and wildlife.

In 1996, fishing, hunting, and wildlife observation produced $1.1 billion in economic output, supported 17,680 jobs, and generated $67.7 million in state tax revenues. Surprisingly, wildlife-watching leads Maine's recreation industries. According to chamber of commerce data, in 1996 nature observers in Maine spent $224.6 million and put 6,020 people to work, generating $111.4 million in wages.

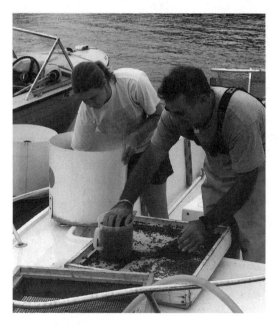

Aquaculture takes many forms. Here, oysters are being graded for size using a mesh screen. *Photo by Bill MacDonald, courtesy of the Island Institute.*

61

Lobstering then and now. The photo below was taken in December 1999, on Monhegan Trap Day, the time when local lobstermen set out traps for the island's special winter season. *Photo by Bill MacDonald, both photos courtesy of the Island Institute.*

Forest-based manufacturing and upcountry tourism contribute an estimated $39.8 million to Maine's tax revenues; recreation revenues provide more than half of this amount. According to the Northeastern Forest Alliance, each thousand acres of usable Maine forest directly supports 1.4 manufacturing jobs and 1.5 forest-based tourism jobs. Both of these woods-based industries provide more than fifty thousand jobs (12 percent of total state employment) and generate a payroll of $888 million (11 percent of the state's payroll).

More than thirty thousand people work in the state's forest-products industry. An additional fourteen thousand jobs are provided by forest-products related support services.

Forest-based manufacturing (stumpage, harvesting, sawmills, pulp and paper, furniture and fixtures, and other wood products) generates a payroll of more than $665 million, resulting in an estimated total economic impact (generated by sales and payroll) of $5.3 billion. Other revenues from Maine's forest products include: 112,000 gallons of maple syrup valued at nearly $1.9 million; more than one million wreaths valued at $6 million; and three hundred thousand Christmas trees worth $5.25 million.

PROFILE

Dottie Paradis was born and raised in Farmington, but left the state in 1973. "My life in Massachusetts became incredibly stressful," she says, "and with my children both grown, I needed a change." She moved back to Maine in May 1999, leaving a successful career in sales to open an ice cream parlor in Cornish. She chose the state for its affordability and the calming effect of a rural location. "I love running my own business and being closer to family," she says, "and I've found people to be friendly and supportive. Nevertheless, I've been lonely at times, and I miss my friends in Massachusetts." Dottie thinks retirement in Maine would be easier because expectations are lower. "Never move alone," she advises. "It's got to be an adventure you can share with someone you can depend on."

Tourism

Tourism is a traditional Maine industry that is still thriving. From small inns to large resorts, trendy restaurants to wharfside lobster pounds, many Mainers make a good living off of vacationers, 70 percent of whom are out-of-staters. In terms of employment, tourism is the largest industry in Maine, with more than 104,000 jobs generated each year and a payroll of $2.3 billion. And many other businesses profit indirectly through the influx of visitors year round. The state is the biggest beneficiary—tax revenues from tourism in 1998 were $168.8 million in sales tax, $88.6 million in personal income tax, and $41.9 million in gasoline tax.

Can you make a decent living in a seasonal industry such as tourism? That's what Dottie Paradis asked herself before she moved to Maine in 1999. "I was expecting a lot more foot traffic," she says of her ice cream parlor in the small inland York County town of Cornish. "I've taken a huge salary cut from what I was making in Massachusetts. But I love running my own business and making my own hours." Many Mainers feel the same way.

For more specifics about tourism in the state, contact the Maine Office of Tourism at 207-623-0363 or see its website at www.mainetourism.com.

A Bevy of Small Businesses

The entrepreneurial spirit is alive and well in Maine. Small businesses of all types seem to thrive. Nearly 90 percent of Maine companies employ fewer than twenty people, and seventy thousand Mainers describe themselves as self-employed. The state sponsors many initiatives to help small businesses and maintains seven Small Business Development Centers.

A good source of information, if you are thinking of starting a Maine business, is Business Answers, an initiative of the Maine Department of Economic and Community Development. Business Answers offers one-stop business licensing, answers questions of all types, and sends out a start-up kit that includes all the forms and information necessary to set up shop. To obtain a kit (and save yourself dozens of calls), send a check for four dollars, payable to the Treasurer, State of Maine, to Business Answers, 59 Statehouse Station, Augusta ME 04333. Or you can call them at 800-872-3838 (within Maine) or 800-541-5872 (from out of state).

Family Ties

Maine also has a high percentage of independently owned family businesses. The Institute for Family-Owned Business at the University of Southern Maine estimates that of the state's fifty thousand businesses, some forty-five thousand are family owned. Some, like Kennebunkport-based Tom's of Maine are first-generation businesses owned and run by their founders. Others, like The Smiling Cow, a retail store overlooking Camden harbor, are into their third generation, and an impressive number of Maine businesses go back as many as four or five generations.

United States Senator Susan Collins, herself the child of a multigenerational Maine business (S.W. Collins Lumber Company in Caribou), is a strong advocate for small businesses. She has sponsored bills providing estate-tax relief for family-owned businesses and farms. She believes family businesses can be the strongest, because family bonds create a strong commitment to employees and communities that might otherwise be lacking.

Camden's Main Street in 1945. Today The Smiling Cow is a third-generation business that is still going strong. *Photo courtesy of Meg Quijano.*

Moving a Business to Maine

A wide range of incentives and benefits are offered to businesses that decide to move to Maine through the Department of Economic and Community Development's Office of Business Development. These programs include business property-tax reimbursements, job and investment tax credits, and sales tax exemptions. Contact the office for more information at 207-287-2656.

Probably the biggest incentives for moving a business here, however, are Maine people themselves. Ask just about any employer in the state, and you'll surely hear that the Maine worker is a highly valued asset. Mainers

BUSINESS AND TRANSPORTATION

- Totaling thirty-two thousand miles, Maine's roads and bridges were ranked seventh-best in the country by a 1996 University of North Carolina survey.
- Interstate 95 runs the length of the state, and Route 1 is the major artery serving the coast.
- More than 450 trucking firms provide intrastate service.
- Maine has a twenty-year highway maintenance and improvement plan.
- Most of Maine is relatively congestion-free; business here is not slowed down by traffic jams.
- The Maine Department of Transportation is doubling the biennial investment in bridges.
- Seven short-line railroad companies operate fourteen hundred miles of track.
- Maine has seven strategically located seaports.
- The largest cargo shipping ports are in Eastport, Searsport, and Portland. They can handle most types of cargo and provide regular service to Europe, Asia, and Canada.
- Eastport is New England's fastest-growing international cargo port, annually shipping more than two hundred thousand tons.

MAINE WORKFORCE FACTS

- According to national standards, 83 percent of Maine's work-force is skilled.
- High school or post-secondary degrees are held by 83 percent of the one hundred thousand job seekers registered for work.
- Maine recently ranked number one in the nation in increasing its level of investment in higher education.
- More than 60 percent of Maine students pursue post-secondary education each year.
- Maine is the first state in the country to have every school and library—nearly twelve hundred facilities—linked by an advanced telecommunications technology called Frame Relay.

are well known for their strong work ethic and commitment to delivering top-quality work. Labor disputes here are rare—in fact, only one Maine company experienced a work stoppage in the past three years.

In addition, Maine offers a comprehensive workforce-development system should the need to upgrade worker skills arise. When businesses in the state venture into an area that requires new skills among their workers, Maine's technical schools and universities work closely to provide the needed training and education.

The Finance Authority of Maine

Maine's business-finance agency is the Finance Authority of Maine. FAME supports start-up and expanding businesses by working closely with Maine banks to improve access to capital. It offers a wide array of programs, ranging from traditional loan guarantees for small and large businesses to tax credits for investments in dynamic manufacturing or export-related firms. FAME has also established taxable and tax-exempt bond financing programs that provide loans to creditworthy firms at very favorable rates and terms. Some of the authority's many programs are:

- The Commercial Loan Insurance Program
- Export Financing Services
- Investment Banking Service
- Maine Seed Capital Tax Credit
- Occupational Safety Loan Program
- Plus 1 Computer Loan Program
- Rapid Response Guarantee
- Regional Economic Development Revolving Loan Program
- Small Business and Veterans' Small Business Loan Insurance Program
- Small Enterprise Growth Fund Bond Financing Programs

For more comprehensive information, including eligibility criteria, please call 207-623-3263 or visit FAME's Web site at www.famemaine.com.

Maine in the Global Marketplace

According to the Maine Department of Economic and Community Development, Maine businesses are participating in the global marketplace in record numbers, exporting nearly $1.5 billion worth of goods a year. International exports are growing, and Maine is increasing its profile as a trading partner with the Canadian Maritimes.

The Maine International Trade Center offers businesses and organizations international assistance working to expand the state's economy through increased international trade in goods and services and related activities such as trade missions, training programs, and conferences. For more information, check out its website at www.mitc.com.

Working in the Arts

The Maine Arts Commission does not specifically help artists relocate to Maine, but they do have a number of services in place for resident artists. Four programs are available: the Individual Artist Fellowship Program, the Traditional Arts Apprenticeship Program, the Maine Artist Roster, and the Maine Artist Registry. There is a formal application process, with paperwork due annually on February 2.

The commission's newest initiative, the Contemporary Artist Development Program, was adopted in June 1999. As an umbrella for a variety of services, this program provides reliable information, training, and funding support that responds to the artist's particular discipline, career stage, and professional aspirations.

Maine also supports an innovative "one percent for art" program, which sets aside an amount equal to one percent of the construction budget in a new or renovated public building to purchase original works of art. For further information on funding, residencies, or employment in all disciplines, contact the Maine Arts Commission at 207-287-2750, or visit its website at www.mainearts.com.

Living Here, Working Elsewhere

With Maine's superior telecommunications system, plus good airports, fax machines, and next-day delivery services, it's hard to think of a job that can't be done here. Given this same scenario, it's possible to imagine many situations involving folks who live here, but actually service clients somewhere else.

Lafayette Center in Kennebunk, the administrative building for Tom's of Maine, international manufacturer of natural personal-wellness products. *Photo by Herb Swanson, courtesy of Tom's of Maine.*

"Neither of us works in Maine," says Jan Njaa, a graphic designer who recently moved with her family to Belfast. "David's a pilot, and he flies out of Minneapolis, and my clients are still in Chicago. We needed to make sure David would have a fairly easy commute to the airport, and Bangor turns out to be very convenient. I needed access to good Internet service and overnight deliveries for my business. Maine's got it all."

Lynda and Thad Chilton may have moved themselves to Maine, but their new business is firmly rooted back in the Washington, D.C. area. "We combined our years of experience as graphic designers and marketers and started our own company here. Our area has high-speed cable Internet access, printers, copywriters, multimedia and web providers, and all the other support people we needed to run a successful business and keep our clients in Washington happy."

Attorney Dana Strout moved east from Colorado. Although his office is located here, his clients are still in the Rocky Mountains. "It's much more profitable for me to work out of state. I can charge more, for one thing, plus it's easier to practice law in Colorado. The Maine judicial system in my opinion is antiquated and disrespectful of lawyers' time. In Colorado, I can do hearings by telephone, and I can send pleadings, briefs, and motions by fax. It's far more convenient to practice law there."

Strout travels back to Colorado to meet with clients nine or ten times a year. "It's actually less traveling than what I did when I lived there," he says. His move to Maine in 1994 was, in fact, a homecoming. "I'm a Mainer. I was born in Lewiston and grew up in Livermore Falls, and I've got more relatives in Maine than you can shake a stick at." He hadn't lived in the state since his teens and is happy to be back. "The lifestyle and the people here are great. I missed Maine terribly. In Denver, I was robbed ten times in fourteen years. It was time to come home."

4 Finding a Home

> *"When we moved from Silicon Valley to midcoast
> Maine, we made an even trade on radio reports—
> California traffic reports for Maine weather reports.
> But we sold our California house for ten times what
> we paid for a 150-acre hilltop farm overlooking
> mountains, lakes, and Penobscot Bay."*
> — Dr. Robert M. Metcalfe*

Maine is a rich mixture of architectural styles and types of dwellings: grand old sea captain's homes gazing out to the ocean, elegant Federals lining a village square. There are raised ranches where yards are strewn with toys, and tidy capes in new subdivisions. Picturesque villages shelter lobster shacks stacked high with traps, and comfortable condominiums with water views. You'll find quiet cabins lining lakefronts and cozy apartments topping downtown shops. There are gleaming new retirement villages as well as trailers that have seen better days. And Maine is home to new houses of every imaginable design: modern, post and beam, solar, and manufactured.

Older Homes Abound

Few states have as many different types of houses as Maine, according to a 1999 report from the Maine State Housing Authority, and few states have as many historic homes. Almost 35 percent of Maine's homes were built before 1940, representing tangible ties to the past that few states can match. They are part of a landscape that, in many cases, seems to have changed little over time—proud white Colonials, extravagant Victorians, rambling farmhouses with attached outbuildings and lofty red barns.

----

*Technology pundit Dr. Robert M. Metcalfe, conversation with author.

John P. Nichols, one of Searsport's most financially successful sea captains, went to sea at age eleven and took charge of his own ship when only twenty-one years old. He commissioned this house, one of the finest Italianate-style homes in Waldo County, upon his retirement. *Photo courtesy Maine Historic Preservation Commission.*

According to the Maine Historic Preservation Commission, nearly twelve hundred properties in Maine—many of them private residences—are listed in the National Register of Historic Places. There are 130 historic districts in Maine, each with dozens—or hundreds—of properties. Portland, Castine, Bangor, and Bath all have large historic areas, as do Rockland, Farmington, Norway, Houlton, Belfast, and Thomaston. Even Maine's more remote corners—Chesuncook Village, in Piscataquis County, for instance, a lakeside community that can only be reached by boat—have homes of significant historical importance.

Maine has scores of Federal, Greek Revival, Italianate, Queen Anne, Shingle Style, and Colonial Revival-Style homes, but it also contains large numbers of Post–World War II ranch houses. Architectural historian Kirk Mohney says that most of the state's communities exhibit a variety of styles, however he notes that the St. John River Valley is unique because of the distinctive early houses built there by Acadian settlers.

The Maine Historic Preservation Commission conducts surveys to identify important historic properties, and keeps an extensive library relating to technical preservation matters. Should you fall in love with an old Maine house, the folks at the commission may have some material relating to it, or they may be able to put you in touch with someone who does. And don't forget local historical societies—often fascinating sources of information.

For further data on historic homes (or to see if an old Maine house meets the National Register criteria) contact the experts at Maine Historic Preservation Commission, 55 Capitol Street, 65 State House Station, Augusta, Maine, 04345-0065. Their telephone number is: 207-287-2132. The website for the commission is: http://janus.state.me.us/mhpc/.

New Homes: To Build or Buy?

Home construction in Maine is on the rise, especially in the southern parts of the state. The value of residential contracts for construction in Maine increased by 7.9 percent in 1997 and surged to 28.3 percent in 1998, and contractors have been very busy since. Maine leads New England in the rate of housing permit growth, with 40 percent of Maine's construction dollars going toward residential development. While this has made builders happy, not everyone is enamored with all of the new growth. Communities around Maine have begun to address the specter of sprawl, taking preventative steps to keep their precious open space and the character of their towns.

Despite the building boom, you may find it difficult to purchase a new home, depending on where in Maine you look. In the fastest-growing parts of the state, demand for new homes far exceeds supply.

PROFILE

David and Jan Njaa moved to Maine in 1999, fifteen years earlier than they'd originally planned. "Even though we loved Chicago, every time we left Maine we looked at each other and wondered why we were going back. There is no other place we feel so in love with or connected to," explains Jan. The Njaas love the landscape of Maine, the people they've met, and the low crime rate. "We love looking out the window and not seeing a brick wall." Jan advises those interested in Maine to "visit during the off months, so you know what it looks like at its worst. If you can make a living here, do it sooner rather than later. There is so much available to have a life rich in nature, culture, and community."

"There's not a big stock of newer homes available in Maine," notes Ellis Cohn, a real-estate broker in the Pine Tree State since the late 1970s and owner of Jaret & Cohn Real Estate, which represents properties in the mid-coast. Demand is high, particularly around Portland and along parts of the coast. From 1990 to 1997, the Greater Portland region added almost six thousand households, with housing production barely keeping pace.

Many newcomers—especially retirees—decide to build houses in Maine, some because they are seeking special views, others because they desire certain amenities not usually found in older homes, still more because they want to build the dream house for which they've long planned. Maine is one of the few places left in the country with reasonably priced shoreland still available.

"It took us twelve years of coming up on weekends from New York to build our house," says Allie Lou Richardson, of Islesboro. "It was worth it, because we wanted to be on the water."

Marlene Kinlin, who moved to Jonesport from Massachusetts, echoes her sentiments: "My husband and I chose Maine for peace of mind as well as the gorgeous, affordable seaside property." The Kinlins retired to Maine in 1994 and built a home with views of lobster buoys and spruce-topped islands.

One thing to remember when considering a coastal site for your dream home, though, is Maine's shoreland zoning law. This regulation places restrictions on a structure's proximity to a body of water, on the clearing of vegetation near the shore, and on types of buildings that can be located on the immediate coast. More information on the law can be found at any town office.

NEW HOUSING STYLES

While Maine has a varied mix of housing styles, there are some that seem to naturally fit into the landscape. Cottage and Shingle Style houses, post-and-beam homes, Capes, and even homes built of Maine cedar logs look quite at home.

The Richardsons of Islesboro chose to build a post-and-beam house, a style characterized by large open spaces and cathedral ceilings combined with the beauty of exposed wood. According to Paul Meynell, of Acadia Post & Beam in Sorrento, this type of construction is a favorite among retirees and young families alike.

Post-and-beam homes feature timber framing and are energy efficient.
Photo courtesy of Rockport Post & Beam.

"Post-and-beam construction has been around for over four thousand years," Meynell says. "The timbers come together using rugged mortise-and-tenon joinery secured with wooden pegs. Most structures over a hundred years old still standing today boast some form of post-and-beam construction.

"I think this type of house suits Maine because of its beauty and authenticity. Plus they are energy efficient and comfortable homes."

Log homes are another popular choice for new residents. One company, Maine Cedar Log Homes, located in Windham, has manufactured this style since 1926. Their homes feature hand-shaved white cedar logs for a natural look with low maintenance, and R-26 walls for energy efficiency.

CHOOSING A BUILDER

If you decide to build, keep in mind that buying land within the traditional village setting, on established roads, will help keep Maine from succumbing to the suburban sprawl that is eating away at much of the U.S.

Whatever style of house you consider, it's wise to take the time necessary to carefully choose your construction team. Mark DeMichele, of Maine Coast Construction in Camden, offers these tips:

- Set aside a minimum of 10 percent of your total budget during the planning stages to give yourself the ability to consider upgrades in materials or compensate for other undetermined costs as the new home takes shape.
- Get the best value for your construction dollar by interviewing architects and builders. Check their financial and client references and look at their past projects and works in progress.
- Choose a "team" that can best assist you in achieving your specific goals within your budget. Remember, the whole process is about working, communicating, and making sound decisions together.
- Another important consideration is your building site. "One formidable surprise that's often found when building in Maine is the condition of and difficulty in developing building sites. Land with the presence of ledge and rock, extreme slopes, poor drainage, and environmentally sensitive issues require more costly solutions for development. Be sure the builder you choose is aware of issues associated with site development and can suggest appropriate steps to surmount specific obstacles."

MANUFACTURED HOUSING

Approximately 13.6 percent of Maine's housing stock is mobile homes, the highest rate in New England. Mobile homes—single and double-wide— have played a big role in Maine's housing growth in the last decade, with one mobile home added for every two site-built homes. Affordability plays a big part: they are a relatively inexpensive match for the relatively inexpensive landscape. The average price of a new double-wide home (not including the land) was $43,000 in 1997.

Since national standards were developed in 1976, mobile homes have become safer and better built. As a result, loans for mobile homes are available on terms only slightly more expensive than those for site-built homes. New mobile home insurance policies are also available.

Another type of manufactured housing is the modular home. Unlike mobile homes, which are placed on a cement slab, modular homes are built on a poured cement foundation and look similar to stick-built structures. They can be custom built to suit just about any style: Cape Cod, ranch, and even Colonial.

Al Benner, of East Holden, has been in the manufactured-housing business for thirty-four years. He says modular homes are popular—particularly with first-home buyers—because they are affordable and can be readily financed. "A modular home runs about 15 to 20 percent less than a stick-built or traditional house, and they can be constructed in five weeks' time or less," he notes. Quality has improved dramatically over the years, too, says Benner. "Maine was the first state to create a construction code for manufactured housing, which became a model for other states. It used to be that banks didn't want to finance these homes, but as the code has improved, so has the quality."

The Maine Manufactured Housing Board regulates the industry in Maine as it relates to construction safety, parts, and licensing of mobile and modular home manufacturers, dealers, and mechanics. By law, every municipality must allow manufactured homes to be installed in their town or city. However, Patrick S. Ouillette, Executive Director of the MMHB, notes that zoning restrictions are acceptable by state law and are common. For more information, call the Maine Manufactured Housing Board at 207-624-8612. Contact Al Benner Homes at 1-800-287-1071 or visit the website at http://byme.com/bennerhomes/.

Home Inspections

Whether you are interested in a vintage Victorian or a new ranch, a thorough examination of the house from top to bottom is crucial. Love is blind, so it's a good idea, especially with older Maine homes, to go over the place thoroughly. An experienced and impartial home inspector can gave a visual examination of the physical structure and systems of a home, examining the heating system, the interior plumbing and electric system, the roof and visible insulation, walls, ceiling, floors, windows and doors, the foundation, and the basement. Although Maine does not have a termite problem like southern states, carpenter ants can be a nuisance. A professional can check for these and other pests, as well as conduct tests to check for the presence of harmful chemicals or elements.

This elegant Queen Anne–style home in Skowhegan is one of the finest in the state. It was built in 1887 for Samuel Wadsworth Gould, a local lawyer and busi-nessman. *Photo courtesy of Maine Historic Preser-vation Commission.*

Which tests are important in Maine? In addition to drinking water tests, experts recommend lead and asbestos screening for homes built prior to 1978. Testing for radon, a naturally occuring gas produced by the break-down of uranium in soil, rock, and water, is also important in this granite-rich state. Radon may be released into your home through air and water, and according to the Surgeon General, is a leading cause of lung cancer. (The EPA publishes a number of informative documents about radon for con-sumers. Many of the radon related booklets are available through the EPA's website, www.epa.gov/radonpro/, or through state radon offices.)

Your real-estate professional will know licensed inspectors in the area and can help put you in contact with one. If you can, it's wise to be there while he or she conducts the inspection and see firsthand any problems or concerns. Following the inspection, you'll receive a written report describ-ing the house's condition in more detail than you ever thought possible.

Retirement Communities

The newest developments on the housing scene are retirement communities. As of March 2000, there were thirty-five privately developed retirement cen-ters in Maine offering living units of various types—cottages, independent apartments, and facilities with assisted-living and long-term care options. More units are being built all the time. See Appendix 5 for addresses and other details.

Located both along the coast and inland, retirement villages offer maintenance-free living and a lively social scene. Many are affiliated with health-care providers through which residents can quickly gain access to an entire continuum of care.

Retirement communities are set up in several ways. For instance, at Avalon Village, a retirement community on the banks of the Penobscot River only five minutes from Bangor, the home buyer receives a share of stock representing the value of the residence. The equity in your new home belongs to you and your estate. In contrast, Schooner Estates, a retirement community nestled in a country setting near Auburn, offers independent-living apartments, assisted-living studio apartments, and a residential-care living center, but all are rental properties.

Condominiums

After years of little activity, the market for condominiums in southern Maine is once again booming. Sales of condos are stronger than ever, say real estate brokers, and it is difficult to find condo properties at any price. Developers have begun to respond to the demand for these low-maintenance homes, popular with both first-time buyers and retirees. If you are in the market for a condo, your timing may be right. The next few years will undoubtedly bring more condominium projects, especially in the southern part of the state.

In other parts of Maine, condos are rarer than snowstorms in July. "You just don't see that type of housing in much of Maine," says a developer. "This state is still heavily weighted toward traditional home ownership."

Apartment and House Rentals

In fact, the heads of three out of every four Maine households own their own homes, a remarkable statistic given the economic slowdown of the early 1990s. Depending on the community, renting a home or apartment in Maine can be next to impossible. High-growth areas, such as the coast and southern Maine, face a rental deficit that builders and municipal planners are trying to address. In communities where growth is not so rapid, rentals are both available and generally very reasonable.

Renters are in the minority in Maine, and sometimes feel at a disadvantage. "While I've met fabulous landlords here, there are no standardized landlord-tenant rules in Maine," says Dottie Paradis of Cornish. "I've never paid for water or sewer while renting in Massachusetts."

Buying Real Estate in Maine

So you've spotted a gracious Federal-style home in a friendly community, or found a piece of land just right for that Shingle-Style cottage of your dreams. Now the time has come to negotiate and seal the deal.

Many Maine real estate brokers offer websites with helpful information on finding property (try the Maine Multiple Listing Service or www.realestate maine.com) as well as links to other Maine sites of interest. The following information is distilled from the "Frequently Asked Questions" section of the website of Camden Real Estate (www.camdenre.com), with special thanks to my favorite Maine lawyer, Ed Doudera.

REAL ESTATE BROKERS

Maine recognizes three levels of real-estate professionals—brokers, associate brokers, sales agents, and timeshare agents—and all must be licensed by the Maine Real Estate Commission. Brokers have the most experience and training; agents must work under a designated broker.

A good real-estate professional is an invaluable asset when moving anywhere. In Maine, they seem to often go above and beyond the call of duty, serving in many instances as a bridge to the new community. "Our real-estate agent tried to inform us about Belfast as much as possible," says Jan Njaa, who moved here in 1999. "He really helped us make a smooth transition from Chicago to Maine, and even went the extra mile to show us around once we arrived."

Since a real-estate transaction may involve one or more real-estate licensees, it's important to know whose interests are represented by each agent. At one time, brokers were understood to represent the seller, and this was true regardless of whether the broker was the listing agent or the selling agent. Today, that's not always the case. The Maine Real Estate Commission gives this advice: Buyers and sellers should not assume that an agent is acting on their behalf unless they have contracted with that person

HOUSING COSTS IN THE BATH-BRUNSWICK AREA

Like much of Maine, the midcoast region encompassing the city of Bath and the growing towns of Brunswick and Topsham features a tremendous variety of residential housing. Here's a look at some of the choices, along with typical costs in 1999.

Type of House	Average Selling Price
Condominium	$60,000 and up
Planned Unit Development	$80,000 to $120,000
Older Housing Stock	$70,000 to $150,000
New Custom Construction	$200,000 to $350,000
Waterfront Location	$250,000 to $600,000
Seasonal Cottages	$70,000 to $150,000
One or two-bedroom apartment,furnished	$400 per month

to represent them. Maine law also provides that a real-estate licensee may represent both the buyer and seller in the same transaction, but only with the informed written consent of both parties.

Increasingly common in Maine is the Buyer Agent or "buyer's broker," a professional who helps a buyer find suitable property and to acquire it at the most advantageous price and terms. Buyer's brokers can be a real boon to people hoping to relocate to Maine from far away because they're familiar with the local market and can do much of the legwork.

WHAT *IS* A BUYER'S BROKER?

The traditional way real-estate brokers make money is to list—and then sell—as many houses as possible. Buyer's brokers, who represent folks looking for property, are turning that logic upside down.

"All I do is represent buyers in search of property," says Bob Fenton of Belfast. "I'm an exclusive buyer agent, so I can offer people an unbiased approach to real estate because I have no stake in them buying one property over another. And rather than focusing on one community like a traditional

81

broker, I can give out-of-state clients a good overview of what's available in my area."

Some brokers are dual agents, and will represent both buyers and sellers, but Bob Fenton sees such a relationship as a conflict of interest. "I don't think it makes sense," he reasons. "After all, would you hire a doctor who did podiatry one day and brain surgery the next?"

CLOSING COSTS

What does it cost to buy property in Maine? Here is a breakdown of costs to give you an idea.

Bank Charges: Banks require an application fee (approximately $350) to begin processing your mortgage request. This fee is applied to your closing costs, which generally include:

- Loan commitment fee (depending upon the interest rate charged)
- Underwriting fee: $100
- Document preparation fee: $150
- Recording fees (for the mortgage deed): $30
- Settlement agent fee: $300
- Credit report: $25
- Appraisal: $300
- Flood zone determination: $25
- Prepaid interest: interest from the date of closing to the day of the month on which your monthly payment will be due.

Real-Estate Tax: In many Maine communities the real estate tax is determined on a tax-year basis running from July 1 through June 30. Make sure your contract provides that real-estate taxes on the property will be prorated as of the date of closing. Generally, taxes for the current year are paid as part of the closing settlement process, even if some portion of the real-estate tax is not yet due. (If a transaction closes before the tax rate for the current year has been established, it is customary to use the previous year's tax figure to do the proration rather than having to make further adjustments once the new tax rate is set. It's a good idea to address this issue in the purchase and sale agreement.)

Attorney's Fees: At closing, purchasers are generally required to provide and pay for a title insurance binder with appropriate endorsements, generally obtained from an attorney. When you apply for financing, the bank will ask whether you want to select your own attorney or have the bank select one.

An attorney selected by the bank represents the bank—not you. Because of this, you may want to select your own attorney to do the title work and to certify title to the bank or to a land title insurance company. As long as the attorney selected meets the bank's requirements for liability insurance, you will not be charged any additional amount in connection with the title work.

Real-Estate Transfer Tax: The state imposes a transfer tax on virtually all transfers of real property. The tax, which is paid by both buyer and seller, is $1.10 per $500, or fractional part thereof, of consideration or value. This tax must be paid at the Registry of Deeds as part of the recording process.

THE TRANSACTION

The process of buying a house in Maine differs from that in many parts of the country, especially out West. Here is a brief overview of the steps involved:

Once you have decided upon your property, your broker will prepare a purchase-and-sale contract that will include a number of standard clauses as well as some prepared with your needs and concerns in mind. Certain types of properties will also require the insertion of specific contract provisions.

For instance, if you are buying a shorefront property, you'll want to require that the seller provide a certificate indicating the condition of the septic system over the past 180 days. Also, you might want to include a clause providing for a review of the purchase-and-sale contract by your attorney before you need to sign.

The purchase-and sale-contract is not a contract until the sellers accept the buyers' offer and sign the agreement themselves. Generally a purchase-and-sale contract has a number of contingencies. The most frequent are: house inspection, financing, water safety test, survey or lot configuration, and radon testing.

What's the role of the real-estate professional during all this give and take? The brokers assist and monitor the activities necessary to fulfill the contingencies and then produce a document indicating when they are fulfilled. Now the buyer's attorney can perform the title examination. The

Located in the Broad Street Historic District in Bethel, this house was once the home and clinic of Dr. John George Gehring, a well-known psychotherapist. It was constructed in 1896. *Photo courtesy Maine Historic Preservation Commission.*

results should be communicated to the buyers at the same time they are communicated to the lender, through a preliminary title certificate or a binder for title insurance.

Once the title work, appraisal, and other documentation required by the bank is assembled and approved by the underwriting department, the transaction is ready to be closed.

TITLE INSURANCE IN MAINE: LENDER'S AND OWNER'S POLICIES

Virtually all banks making residential mortgage loans in Maine now require a title insurance policy to protect their interest in the property, which is generally the original amount of the loan itself.

The basic cost of such lender's title insurance is $1.75 per $1,000 of loan. In addition to the basic premium, certain endorsements are required for different situations. Virtually every transaction requires a "secondary mortgage market endorsement" at a cost of $25 as well as an "environmental protection lien endorsement" also at a cost of $25. Endorsements for variable rate mortgages, for condominiums, or for manufactured housing units also cost $25 each.

The *lender's* title insurance policy offers no protection to the owner even though the owner pays for the policy. If a title related issue arises, for instance an ancient right of way that has not been mentioned in the chain of deeds researched prior to the purchase, the title insurer will not step in, for until the lender suffers an actual loss (foreclosure) it has no duty to intervene.

84

Ten or fifteen years ago, title insurance in Maine was relatively uncommon and many purchasers and their attorneys didn't bother with *owners'* policies. Today, though, experts say it's a good idea. Title insurance protects your investment while you own it and also covers any warranty covenants you may offer in a deed to subsequent purchasers. If any of the covered situations arise, the title insurer will either correct the problem or reimburse you for insured losses up to the amount of the policy. You'll also be defended against any lawsuit attacking the title. The cost for title insurance is a one-time premium.

LOANS

According to the Maine State Housing Authority, there is no shortage of capital for any form of housing activity in Maine for families with adequate incomes and credit eligibility. Home improvement loans from Maine banks totaled an estimated $130 million in 1997, but this represents only a fraction of home improvement activity, say experts. As with other parts of the country, a more popular way to finance home improvements is through an equity line of credit.

Heating Your Home

Even the Maine State Housing Authority admits that energy costs are high. "Electricity is expensive here," says Marlene Kinlin, who moved to Jonesport from Massachusetts in 1994. The high cost of heating a home is particularly unsettling for those who relocate from outside the Northeast, and many new residents are dismayed to find that natural gas, while now generally available inland, is not an option everywhere.

Far and away the most popular fuel in Maine is oil. "The cheapest thing is Number Two fuel oil," says Willard Wight, whose family has been in the fuel business in the midcoast since 1899. "Everything is on the expensive side—electricity is high, and so is propane. Kerosene, also called K-1, is a more refined oil used in certain types of units, but it's pricey. By far, the most efficient fuel in the state is oil."

Efficient, but in recent memory, expensive. In January and February 2000, the prices New England residents paid for oil reached their highest levels in at least twenty years when a number of conditions coincided to boost demand and limit supplies. A sudden surge of cold weather that moved in across New England and much of the Eastern seaboard, as well as a shortage of crude oil coming into the Northeast from overseas, combined to send retail prices skyward. Rates of $1.70 per gallon were all the more shocking when compared with 1999 prices, which were well below $1 per gallon.

The issue of Maine's dependence on overseas oil is a much-debated topic, particularly once the snow flies. The idea of creating an oil reserve for the Northeast is one response to shortages; alternative types of fuel are another. Approximately twenty-two thousand consumers currently are natural gas customers in Maine, and there are three proposals to construct natural gas pipelines and storage facilities in the Maine coastal zone. The largest of these projects would link gas resources offshore of Nova Scotia to the United States natural gas transmission system.

While solar energy warms other parts of the country, its future in Maine is still somewhat cloudy. "We can't rely on the amount of sunlight here," says Willard Wight, "And solar panels and the like are quite costly to install."

Woodstoves, however, are a common fixture in most Maine homes. Some households heat solely with wood (and to a lesser extent, coal) while others rely on woodstoves to supplement or back up a primary source of heat. Firewood isn't inexpensive—it usually runs between $100 and $130 a cord—cut, split, and delivered. It can be purchased in longer lengths for significantly less, if you're willing to do the final cutting yourself. How much wood does a woodstove burn in a typical Maine winter? An average homeowner using wood along with another fuel source will burn about two cords. Those using wood alone can expect to burn between four and five cords by the time warmer weather rolls around.

Settling In

"I write about Maine because it's what I know best, but I also write about Maine because it's the place I love best."

—STEPHEN KING*

Most new residents find Maine communities surprisingly easy to slide into. "Our neighbors, even in this small coastal community, are friendly, and there's a real willingness to help others," says Carol Doherty-Cox of Port Clyde.

"I wish I had known how easy the transition would be," says Barry Hurtt, who was recruited from a New Jersey medical center to direct the Northeast Health Foundation in Rockport. "Warm and helpful associates, neighbors, and community members set to rest the rumors of a cold and standoffish population."

Many new residents are amazed by the investment of time and energy Mainers make in their towns and cities. "I was surprised by the degree to which people are actively involved in the development of the community here," says Kristy Scher, who moved from Los Angeles to the midcoast in 1999. "It has been really wonderful and inspiring to see and work with a community of people who are so committed to living in a healthy, happy society. People are much less jaded in Maine—it's refreshing."

Voter Registration

Voting is an important part of Maine citizenship. Turnout is generally strong, with the state consistently placing in the top five states—and often garnering first place—for voter participation. Presidential election years draw

---

*Stephen King, on Simon and Schuster's website to promote *Bag of Bones,* quoted in *Stephen King Country,* by George Beahm, Running Press, 1999.

Voting in many towns still involves the use of an old-fashioned ballot box. *Photo courtesy of the* Camden Herald.

the most Maine voters, with an average of 65.8 percent of citizens casting ballots since 1980. Gubernatorial election years rank second with an average of 52.6 percent since 1978.

Maine is noted for its progressive voting laws. Maine was among the first states to adopt mail-in voter registration (possible up to two weeks before the election), same-day voter registration (bring proof of residence to voting place), and a motor voter program, which permits the Bureau of Motor Vehicles personnel to register voters. Maine law makes absentee ballots easily accessible—just contact your town office or city hall. Maine law also has special provisions to make registering to vote easier for those who have nontraditional residences. Most recently, the Maine Legislature protected the voting rights of stalking victims, by requiring their addresses be kept confidential.

Your Town Office or City Hall

People in Maine value local services, and pay for them (some think dearly) through local taxes.

Town offices such as the Cornish Town Hall are at the heart of Maine's small communities. *Photo by Ernie Rose.*

Spectators line the street to watch Camden's Memorial Day Parade. Community celebrations like this are a colorful part of small-town life. *Photo courtesy of the Camden Herald.*

Nevertheless, your local town or city hall is a convenient source of just about any type of information you need. In addition, clerks at the office can issue landfill permits, birth and death certificates, dog licenses, fishing licenses, hunting licenses, building permits, motor bike permits, and permits for snowmobiles, boats, and ATVs. The town office or city hall is also where you pay your annual automobile excise tax.

Driver's Licenses

The Maine Bureau of Motor Vehicles (also known as the Division of Motor Vehicles) has offices in thirteen locations across the state where Maine driver's licenses are issued. A Maine license is valid for six years. To obtain one, you'll need your out-of-state license and one other form of identification. Unless you want to brush up on your driving skills, don't worry about studying—written tests are no longer necessary. (A national security check will be performed on your driving record.) You will be required to take an eye test, though, and pay a forty-dollar charge.

Maine is in the midst of a switch to digital licenses. Depending on which branch office you visit, you may receive the new high-tech card. With Maine's staggered renewal cycle and the state's eight hundred thousand licensed drivers, officials estimate that it will take until 2007 to completely replace all Maine driver's licenses with the more modern models.

BUREAU OF MOTOR VEHICLES LOCATIONS

Open 8 a.m. to 5 p.m., Monday through Friday. Closed on all legal holidays.

Augusta	285 State St.	207-287-3330
Bangor	Airport Mall	207-942-1319
Calais	204 North St.	207-454-2175
Caribou	159 Bennett Dr., Suite 1	207-492-9141
Ellsworth	24 Church St.	207-667-9363
Kennebunk	63 Portland Road, Suite 4	207-985-4890
Lewiston	124 Canal St.	207-783-5370
Mexico	Mexico Shopping Plaza	207-369-9921
Portland	312 Canco Rd.	207-822-6400
Rockland	212 New County Rd. (Thomaston)	207-596-2255
South Portland	364 Maine Mall Rd.	207-822-0730
Springvale	185 Main St., Rt. 109	207-490-1261
Topsham	49 Topsham Fair Mall Rd.	207-725-6520

Vehicle Registration and Inspection

Cars are registered annually on a staggered basis. Generally, registrations expire one year from the month issued. You need evidence of auto insurance (see "Insurance," page 94) and your annual excise-tax payment to register a car. Registration can be done in person at a BMV office or through the mail. (Bureau of Motor Vehicles, Vehicle Services Division, 29 State House Station, Augusta, Maine 04333-0029.) Most municipalities also issue registrations and plates, so check first with your city or town to see if they participate in this program. If you choose to register your car in your new hometown, you may need to pay a small additional service charge, but since you'll have to go to city hall or the town office to pay your automobile excise tax anyway, it's convenient to renew the registration renewal at the same time.

One interesting aspect of motor vehicle registration in Maine is that no notice of expiration or need for renewal is sent. Many a newcomer and old resident alike has sheepishly accepted a summons for driving an unregistered vehicle! Perhaps for this reason, a new pilot program for electronic registration renewal is underway in several municipalities. If the idea of on-line registration appeals to you, check to see if your community is one of the test cases for this new program.

Maine also requires an annual vehicle safety inspection. Most auto repair shops are also licensed inspection stations.

Registering Your Boat

Whether your taste runs to quiet kayaks, speedy J-24 sailboats, or steady fishing boats, there are plenty of ponds, lakes, rivers, and quiet coastal coves to explore. The Maine Department of Inland Fisheries & Wildlife in Augusta is the central office for boat registrations and registration records, but many municipal tax collectors or town clerks (and a few businesses) can do the job as well. If you are registering a watercraft at the Augusta office or in a town other than your own, you must first pay your annual excise tax in your town of legal residence. You must show the tax receipt in order to register your watercraft at another location.

Do all watercraft need to be registered? Motorboats of any size and non-motorized boats sixteen feet and over do require registration, and your town office can give you the particulars. Another good source of boating information is http://janus.state.me.us/ifw/rv/boatlaws99.htm. This site, maintained by Inland Fisheries and Wildlife, offers registration details as well as tips on boating safety, a boating supplies checklist, a list of which ponds and lakes prohibit personal watercraft and motorized boats, and much more.

SOCIAL SECURITY OFFICES

- Auburn 207-782-5157
- Augusta 207-622-8348
- Bangor 207-990-4530
- Biddeford 207-282-5956
- Portland 207-780-3536

- Presque Isle 207-764-3771
- Rockland 207-596-6633
- Rumford 207-364-3731
- Waterville 207-872-2723

The toll free number for all Social Security offices is 1-800-772-1213

License Plates

Maine began issuing registration plates in 1905, with the state's first and only slogan "Vacationland" appearing on the plate in 1936. Until very recently, the majority of Maine cars have borne lobster plates, but passionate citizen input (and a law requiring the design of plates be changed every eight to twelve years) has made the lobster license plate obsolete. The new plates have a fresh design centered on the state bird, the chickadee.

New residents receive two chickadee plates upon registration, unless specialty plates are requested. While some specialty plates honor veterans or University of Maine graduates, a popular one features a loon and funds conservation efforts at state parks. The cost is an additional twenty dollars for a loon or university model, and five dollars for a veteran plate. Vanity plates are available on selected plate types for an additional annual fee of fifteen dollars.

Handicapped plates require a completed medical form that can be obtained from the BMV.

Driving

Because Maine is a rural state, public transportation is largely limited to the big towns and cities. There are no commuter trains or underground subways

GETTING THERE FROM HERE

Place	Mileage from				
	Portland	Bangor	Brunswick	Rockland	Rumford
Augusta	57	77	31	42	57
Boston	111	241	126	189	194
New York City	328	445	340	375	397
Philadelphia	421	537	447	480	502
Chicago	1053	1139	1106	1158	1075
Montreal	266	302	262	295	247

IN-STATE DISTANCES FROM PORTLAND

City	Miles	Kilometers	City	Miles	Kilometers
Augusta	57	92	Kittery	48	77
Bangor	129	208	Machias	205	330
Bar Harbor	162	261	Old Orchard	17	27
Bethel	66	106	Rangeley	118	190
Boothbay			Houlton	247	397
Harbor	56	90	Caribou	299	481
Camden	83	134	Fort Kent	313	504
Eastport	250	402	Madawaska	346	557
Freeport	13	28	Presque Isle	286	460
Greenville	154	248			

in Maine. For most people, living in small towns means either walking for services or driving a car. But as newcomers quickly notice, driving about the state is relatively easy and often very pleasant.

"Driving here is much easier," says Lynda Chilton of Rockport. "There is no traffic and no sprawling generic suburbs. And Maine drivers are courteous. They stop for pedestrians and rarely honk their horns in anger."

Roads—with the exception of the Interstates and U.S. Route 1—are generally lightly traveled and fairly scenic.

A nationwide study released in 1999 reports that the average driver spends eighty-two hours a year in congestion in Los Angeles, seventy-six in the Washington, D.C., area, sixty-nine in Seattle, and sixty-six in Boston. Contrast that with the few minutes or so wait that Maine "traffic" sometimes causes. The only time that Mainers ever have to deal with traffic jams are in the summer in such bottlenecks as the Bath and Wiscasset bridges and at various toll-booths on the Maine Turnpike.

"I have such a hard time driving back in New Jersey now," says Dan Barnstein of Bath. "The gridlock and road rage have only increased since we left five years ago. When people here complain about the traffic on Route 1, I just chuckle. It's so much more pleasant in Maine."

Despite the lack of public mass transit, those needing transportation assistance will find it. Services providing rides for seniors to doctors' offices, clinics, dining centers, government offices, and pharmacies are available even in the quietest communities. In Androscoggin County, for example, Community Concepts, Inc., offers free transportation to medical appointments for qualified residents. The Department of Transportation's Office of Passenger Transportation has a website listing public and fixed-route transportation providers by county (www.state.me.us/mdot/opt/transit/transit), or check with local town offices for specifics.

Automobile Laws

Maine has some of the toughest laws in the country regarding operating under the influence (OUI). The legal blood alcohol level is low—.08 percent—roughly equal to one cocktail consumed in an hour. (In some states the blood-alcohol level is .10.) And punishment for drivers deemed inebriated is swift and thorough: arrest at the scene, followed by courtroom penalties that include fines and license suspensions. Repeat offenders do jail time and risk losing their vehicle along with their license.

Maine has several new progressive automobile laws as well. Headlights must be on when using windshield wipers. Drivers must stop for pedestrians within any part of a marked crosswalk that is not regulated by a traffic light. Seatbelts are mandatory for all occupants in a car. And parents must follow safety precautions for children riding in automobiles. (See Chapter 9, Family Life.)

Car Insurance

The Bureau of Insurance notes that new residents should be aware of the state's financial responsibility law for car insurance. You cannot register your car in Maine without showing proof of insurance. Keep a proof-of-insurance card in your vehicle, too, because if you are ever stopped by a law officer, you will be asked to produce it.

The minimum limits (which all licensed insurance agents know) are $50,000 for the injury to or death of any one person; $100,000 for one accident resulting in injury to or death of more than one person; and $25,000 for property damage. Medical payment is also required in the amount of $1,000. In addition, the state has mandatory uninsured motorists coverage and the minimum for that is $50,000 per person and $100,000 per accident.

For more information, contact the Insurance Bureau at its toll-free statewide number: 1-800-300-5000, or access its website at www.state.me.us/ pfr/ins/inshome2.

Airports

The old Maine joke that "you can't get there from here" just doesn't ring true in this age of jet flight. If driving is not your style, Maine's airports can whisk you off to wherever in the world you desire. Smaller airports offer connecting flights to the state's international terminals as well as the chance to see beautiful scenery from the air. Many communities offer charter flight services as well.

Incredible as it may seem for travelers accustomed to airport confusion, crowds, and chaos, leaving on a jet plane in Maine is a pleasure. Both Portland International Jetport and Bangor International Airport provide true hassle-free flying. Parking is relatively inexpensive and easily available, crowded gates are nonexistent, and personnel are polite and pleasant, not to mention sharp as tacks. Another enjoyable perk: on nine trips out of ten you'll spot someone you know while strolling to the airport lounge. How often does that happen at Logan or JFK?

There are thirty-six airports and landing strips in Maine. Here are some of the key airports, because of their size and/or location. For a complete list, visit the Maine Department of Transportation's website at: www.state.me.us/ mdot/opt/air/air1d.

- *Augusta Airport:* 207-287-3185. Served by: Colgan Air, Pine State Airlines.
- *Bangor International Airport:* 207-947-0384. Served by: Business Express, Continental Express, Delta Airlines, US Air, Delta Connections, Pan Am, Finnair.
- *Bar Harbor Airport:* 207-667-7329. Served by: Colgan Air.

▲ *Portland International Jetport:* 207-772-0690. Served by: Business Express, Continental Express, Delta Airlines, United Airlines, US Air, Pine State Airlines.

▲ *Northern Maine Regional Airport, Presque Isle:* 207-764-2550. Served by: Business Express, US Airways.

▲ *Knox County Regional Airport, Owls Head:* 207-594-4131. Served by: Colgan Air.

AIRLINES SERVING MAINE

▲ *Business Express:* 1-800-345-3400

▲ *Colgan Air:* 1-800-272-5488

▲ *Continental Express:* 1-800-525-0280

▲ *Delta Airlines:* 1-800-221-1212

▲ *United Airlines:* 1-800-241-6522

▲ *USAir:* 1-800-428-4322

Ferries

Living on an island means working around the arrivals and departures of the ferry. "It can be a challenge to find flights out of Portland that will also mesh with the ferry schedule," says Allie Lou Richardson of Islesboro. "We've become very relaxed about it, and I've found that professionals on the mainland are very understanding when I'm occasionally late."

Coastal Mainers are accustomed to taking ferries, whether for work or play. One of my sons remarked as a toddler that he wanted "to own the ferry that came and got your teeth." Only a child living near an island-dotted coast in an entrepreneurial state could hope to buy out the "tooth ferry!"

Good news for islanders and coastal travelers: in the coming years, speedier ferries will ply the high seas. The addition of new routes is part of an exciting plan by the state's Office of Passenger Transportation to increase the use of alternative transportation. A system of ferries linking coastal towns—from Boston to Eastport and into Canada—is being proposed as an alternative to driving Route 1 during the summer.

The Maine State Ferry Service operates most ferries; for general schedule information call 800-491-4883, or check its web page at www.state.me.us/mdot/opt/ferry/ferry.

STATE FERRY SERVICE

↟ *Rockland to Vinalhaven,* 207-863-4421
  Year-round service. 15 miles. Crossing 1 hr., 15 min.

↟ *Rockland to North Haven,* 207-867-4441
  Year-round service. 12.5 Miles. Crossing 1 hr., 10 min.

↟ *Rockland to Matinicus,* 207-596-2202
  23 miles. Crossing 2 hr., 15 min. Ferry service provided one day
  a month (more in summer).

↟ *Lincolnville to Islesboro,* 207-789-5611 or 207-734-6935
  Year-round service. 3 miles. Crossing 20 min.

↟ *Bass Harbor to Swans Island,* 207-526-4273
  Year-round service. 6 miles. Crossing 40 min.

↟ *Bass Harbor to Frenchboro,* 207-244-3254 or 800-491-4883
  8.25 miles. Crossing 50 min.

OTHER FERRIES

↟ *Monhegan Boat Line,* 207-372-8848
  Year-round ferry service to Monhegan from Port Clyde.

↟ *Northumberland/Bay Ferries,* 888-249-7245
  Yarmouth, Nova Scotia, to Bar Harbor, Maine (seasonal).

↟ *Prince of Fundy Cruises,* 800-341-7540
  Yarmouth, Nova Scotia to Portland, Maine (seasonal).

↟ *Casco Bay Lines,* 207-774-7871
  Year-round service to Peaks, Chebeague, Long, Great and Little
  Diamond, and Cliff Islands.

↟ *The Cat,* 888-249-7245.
  High-speed catamaran from Bar Harbor to Yarmouth, Nova Scotia.

Bus Services

Now that buses are smoke-free, they provide a healthy and enjoyable way to
travel without having to take the wheel. You can even take in a movie on
some routes. Here are the bus lines that serve Maine.

↟ *Concord Trailways,* 1-800-639-3317. Service to: Bangor, Bath,
  Belfast, Brunswick, Camden, Damariscotta, Portland, Rockland,
  Searsport, Waldoboro, and Wiscasset.

⚑ *Greyhound Bus Lines*, 1-800-231-2222. Service to: Bangor and Portland.

⚑ *Vermont Transit Lines*, 207-772-6587. Service to: Augusta, Bangor, Brunswick, Lewiston, Portland, and Waterville.

Trains

Passenger rail service is on its way back to Maine. High-speed trains to Boston from Portland are expected to start running at the end of the year 2000 and make the trip in two and a half hours. Amtrak is in the process of upgrading existing freight lines to passenger rail standards, and communities as far north as Rockland are looking for ways to get on board as well.

PROFILE

"We flew up to Bar Harbor to look at post-and-beam houses," remembers Allie Lou Richardson. "And on our return, flew over Islesboro and decided it looked like a great place to live." With a bird's-eye view of the island, the Richardsons began a twelve-year process of building their retirement home. "During that time we were too busy to have any concerns," she says. "The year before we moved, I began to panic. I wondered whether we'd find island living isolating, and I worried about health care and making new friends."

The Richardsons made the move to Islesboro in 1997, and found their fears to be unfounded. "There's plenty to do on the island, and our medical needs are well provided for by the local health center. We don't miss the mainland or New York. We do miss our children," says Allie Lou. "But then, we might move closer to them and they might move to Maine. It's kind of far for our friends to come visit, too." But by and large, the Richardson's move to Maine has surpassed their expectations. "We wish we had done it sooner," Allie Lou says. "We've learned to make do and be much more relaxed."

Former Maine Senator George Mitchell got the project on track in 1993 when he sponsored legislation leading Congress to appropriate $39 million for track improvements. Because the initiative involves three states—Maine, Massachusetts, and New Hampshire—and many miles of old tracks, it has taken years to make Mitchell's dream a reality. But thanks to the perseverance of many dedicated train fans, riding the rails along the coast will be possible once more.

Maine's Office of Passenger Transportation and an organization called TrainRiders Northeast are looking for ways to increase rail travel into the state's interior as well. Plans are in the works for a line connecting Portland to Montreal. By all accounts, it won't be long before residents and tourists alike hear "All Aboard!" once more throughout the state.

Bicycles

Maine is also actively pursuing bicycle travel, including rails-to-trails programs, bike and pedestrian paths, and bicycle tourism. Brunswick's new bike path, which follows the Androscoggin River for two and a half miles, is a huge success, frequented by scores of joggers, walkers, skaters, and yes, cyclists. There's talk of expanding the route to nearby Bath, and some hope it will one day link up with a network of trails that reach as far south as Kittery and as far north as Fort Kent.

Other communities are in the midst of creating bike and pedestrian pathways as well—Bethel, Augusta, and Old Town are just a few. John Balicki, the Bicycle/Pedestrian Coordinator for the Department of Transportation, is working on projects within towns as well as trails that connect communities in regions throughout the state. In the works are three trails—two of which are alongside railroad lines that will again operate—the department hopes to develop within the coming years. Combined, the trails will add up to an impressive 230 or so miles of bicycle routes that will help residents as well as tourists explore Maine from the seat of a bike.

The department provides a list of bike tours currently available in the state at its website at: www.state.me.us/mdot/opt/biketours/biketours. Another tip for bicyclists: Maine's new Bicycle Safety Act requires operators and passengers of bikes under the age of sixteen to wear bicycle helmets.

Health Care

"What about doctors?" One of the biggest concerns of people moving to Maine is the state and availability of health care. "I wondered about the quality of medical care, especially on the island we'd chosen," says Allie Lou Richardson, who moved to Islesboro from suburban New York. Top-notch professionals and state-of-the art facilities are important to all newcomers, especially those planning to raise a family or retire here.

The truth is that high-quality medical care is found throughout Maine for two different, yet complementary reasons: first, hospitals and medical practices still offer the kind of personalized care that has vanished in many big cities; and second, Maine's medical community actively recruits and attracts exceptional professionals from other states who are looking for a more relaxed lifestyle.

What about facilities and equipment? Although hospital costs per case remain less than the national average (and also less than the New England average) Maine's hospitals keep pace with their more expensive cousins in terms of up-to-date equipment and facilities. Administrators credit the state's Certificate of Need law, passed in the mid-1980s, with forcing hospitals to regionalize, promoting efficiency and avoiding duplication of expensive gear.

While the regional approach helps keep costs down, it creates inconvenience for patients when they have to travel forty miles or more for treatments or diagnosis. At times, there's no other option than to get in the car and drive to one of the state's bigger institutions. Although annoying, this narrowing of focus has helped put some places at the forefront in certain specialties.

For instance, Portland's Maine Medical Center is recognized as a national leader in the field of cardiology, with outcomes for heart attack patients among the best in the country. The hospital was recognized by *Fortune* magazine in 1995 as one of the top eight hospitals in America for patients suffering heart attacks. Eastern Maine Medical Center, in Bangor, is another first-rate cardiology hospital. And the Joint Commission on Accreditation of Health Care Organizations ranks Central Maine Medical Center, in Lewiston, in the top ten percent of U.S. hospitals. It's hard to believe that a rural state can have such high-quality medical services, but it's true.

PEDIATRICIAN DANA WHITTEN

A great example of the excellent medical care available in Maine is found in the pediatric practice of Dana Whitten, M.D. Raised in Massachusetts, Dr. Whitten has the kind of glowing resume you'd expect to see in the file of a prestigious big-city institution. His background includes education at Exeter and Harvard, medical training at the University of Pennsylvania School of Medicine, and residencies in Boston in pediatric hematology and oncology. In 1976, Dr. Whitten went from performing bone marrow transplants in Boston to diagnosing diaper rash in Belfast. It was a quality-of-life decision that he's never regretted.

"I hated my one-hour commute into Boston every day," he remembers. "My wife and I have always loved Maine, and we had ties to the state and friends here. We wanted to raise our daughter somewhere safe and beautiful. We came up to Waldo County with our three-year-old and discovered there wasn't a pediatrician in the area. I liked the hospital here in Belfast, so I started a solo practice with a great pediatric assistant—my wife—and fell in love with this kind of medicine."

The Whittens enjoy the benefits of a coastal lifestyle and can be spotted cruising Penobscot Bay in their sailboat. Their presence, in turn, has greatly enriched their midcoast community. "What's different about practicing medicine in Maine is that you know everyone," says Dr. Whitten. "There is a great patient–doctor relationship in a small town. I've kept some of my patients into early adulthood. I see parents everywhere, and they don't hesitate to ask me questions, even in the produce department of the local supermarket." He laughs. "I've even diagnosed a few things over the shopping cart."

His wife Diane, a registered nurse, is the same kind of caring practitioner. Ten years ago, she made a house call to check on a newborn and calm his worried mother. I was that new mom, and I've never forgotten the timeliness of Diane's visit and the competence of her care. It's what medicine in Maine is all about.

EMERGENCY MEDICAL SERVICES

In a vast state, emergency medicine is vital, and in Maine it's improving all the time. Paramedics and emergency medical technicians use the most sophisticated techniques available, and even the smallest of towns boast shiny new ambulances. Training is a constant focus, and even basic first responders are licensed to provide quick, life-saving care, involving the use of equipment like automatic defibrillators, crucial in the event of a heart attack.

Maine uses a unique Statewide Voluntary Trauma System linking hospital facilities with Emergency Medical Services. It's designed to very quickly move an injured person to the most appropriate hospital, no matter in what remote corner the injury may have occurred. And though the state may be rural, the roads tend to be less crammed with traffic, making for quicker emergency transport than in many cities and suburbs.

Maine's "Lifeflight" system, begun in 1998, is a key player in the voluntary Trauma System. Lifeflight's two new helicopters have already flown several hundred missions. One of the helicopters' more famous patients was author Stephen King, who was struck by a car while walking on a rural highway during the summer of 1999. The seriously injured writer was taken to Northern Cumberland Memorial Hospital, a small facility in Bridgton, where he was stabilized, and then flown to Central Maine Medical Center in Lewiston. While the best-selling author certainly has the means to choose any facility in the world for his recovery, all of his treatment—including his follow-up and physical therapy—has taken place in Maine.

HOSPITALS

Thirty-nine acute care and specialty hospitals serve smaller communities throughout Maine. Most are private, nonprofit institutions with volunteer boards of directors made up of members of the very populations they serve. This local involvement keeps hospitals responsive to the community and fosters patient-doctor relationships. After all, it's difficult to give impersonal care to a patient whose son snowboards with yours.

There are also three government-run hospitals in Maine: the Augusta Mental Health Institute and the Bangor Mental Health Institute, as well as the Veteran's Administration Medical Center in Togus.

The small size of Maine's hospitals offers several advantages, one being that treatment often happens more quickly because there aren't as many dis-

Maine Medical Center, in Portland, is the state's busiest community hospital, as well as the area's leading provider of specialized services. MMC's open-heart surgery program is the largest in New England.
Photo courtesy of Maine Medical Center.

tractions. When my daughter required emergency care recently at Penobscot Bay Medical Center in Rockport, a team was working on her before we could even take our jackets off. We knew the doctor on duty, who serves as a Cub Scout leader in town, and were able to call a specialist—another friend—who arrived promptly. While our daughter underwent surgery, my husband and I sat in the hushed waiting room, calm and quiet on a Wednesday night. We felt a rush of emotions, among them gratitude for the speedy, high-quality medical care available to us in our home area.

The state's two tertiary care hospitals are Maine Medical Center in Portland, the largest hospital in northern New England, and Eastern Maine Medical Center in Bangor.

See Appendix 2 for a complete list of hospitals.

MAINE MEDICAL CENTER

Located in the heart of the city, Maine Medical Center serves as a community hospital for the Greater Portland area, as the medical hub for the southern half of the state, and as a center for health research and education for health care professionals. Maine Med includes the Barbara Bush Children's Hospital (which added a brand new inpatient unit in 1998) and Spring Harbor Hospital, a locally owned, not-for-profit mental health resource. Recently, Maine Med was named one of the Top 100 U.S. Cardiovascular Hospitals by HCIA Inc., a national health care information company.

Maine Medical Center is a nonprofit institution dedicated to the highest quality of care possible for all Maine people. Along with additions to the Children's Hospital, Maine Med recently opened a new inpatient facility for the care of adult cancer patients called The Gibson Pavilion. The research arm of the hospital, The Maine Medical Center Research Institute, is in the process of building a new home for its laboratory research divisions. This state-of-the-art facility will allow Maine Medical Center to expand research projects and attract new researchers.

EASTERN MAINE MEDICAL CENTER

Eastern Maine Medical Center (EMMC) is a locally owned and directed facility offering acute, secondary, and tertiary care. Located along the Penobscot River in Bangor, the hospital complex consists of nine modern buildings containing 426 beds. The hospital opened its doors in 1892 as Bangor General Hospital and has provided high-quality health care to residents of greater Bangor and northern and eastern Maine ever since.

EMMC is the largest subsidiary of Eastern Maine Health Care, a system offering a continuum of health services to area residents. The hospital boasts the latest in facilities and equipment, including an extensive emergency unit and a world-class cancer unit. In 1995, EMMC opened a new $6.2-million children's wing, designed with the care and comfort of little patients and their parents in mind.

COMPLEMENTARY MEDICINE

In addition to traditional medicine, Maine offers a growing array of non-traditional and holistic care. Perhaps it is a reflection of the independent nature of Mainers, or their entrepreneurial spirit, but several communities offer a surprising variety of choice in what was once viewed as alternative medicine. In Camden, for instance, three beautifully renovated houses are home to the Wellness Center, offering treatments in massage therapy, acupuncture, and the ancient Japanese healing art of Reiki, to name a few.

Statewide networks of hospice workers help the dying and their families as they go through the physical and emotional hardships of a terminal illness. Homeopathic practitioners across the state treat ailments from allergies to colic using natural substances. Certified nurse midwives and doulas assist in the births of hundreds of healthy babies. And Maine's 450 or so osteopathic physicians are trained and licensed practitioners who embrace a "whole person" approach to medicine that emphasizes the body's ability to heal itself. (Many of these D.O.s are graduates of Maine's medical school, the University of New England College of Osteopathic Medicine in Biddeford.)

Getting the News

Maine has seven daily papers: the *Portland Press Herald,* the *Bangor Daily News,* the *Kennebec Journal* (Augusta), the *Sun Journal* (Lewiston), the *Journal Tribune* (Biddeford), the *Times Record* (Brunswick), and the *Central Maine Morning Sentinel* (Waterville). In addition, more than fifty weeklies—some of them alternatives like Portland's spunky *Casco Bay Weekly*—cover communities from Caribou to Cutler, serving up local issues and news and offering a good taste of town politics and activities. Reading them before relocating provides an excellent window into a particular community. (The award-winning weekly the *Ellsworth American* even offers a free four-week subscription to those interested in Hancock County.) Appendix 3 lists addresses and phone numbers of all the Maine newspapers.

And what about the big city papers? Will moving to Maine mean sacrificing forever the *Wall Street Journal* or the *New York Times*?

While you can probably find your favorite paper on-line these days, stores in most Maine communities do sell major newspapers such as the *Wall Street Journal,* the *New York Times, USA Today* and the *Boston Globe.* Many local libraries subscribe to these papers as well. The only difference you may notice is that out-of-state papers tend to arrive at newsstands a tad later in the morning than in cities farther south.

Several magazines are published in Maine. Here are those which deal exclusively with the state:

⚓ *Down East:* "The Magazine of Maine." Published monthly. Call 1-800-766-1670 for information, or check www.downeast.com.

105

▲ *People, Places and Plants.* Published five times yearly. Call 207-428-4001, or visit the website at www.peopleplacesplants.com.

▲ *Maine Boats and Harbors.* Published five times a year. Call 1-800-565-4951, or visit the website at www.maineboats.com.

▲ *Travel Golf Maine.* Published bimonthly. Call 207-236-6716, or visit the website, www.travelgolfmaine.com.

▲ *Maine Golf Magazine.* Call 207-623-6097, or visit the website at www.mainegolfmagazine.com.

Shopping

In an era in which shopping is ranked one of America's favorite activities, it comes as no surprise that some newcomers cite lack of retail choice as one of the biggest challenges to living in Maine. Indoor malls are few: the Maine Mall in South Portland, the Bangor Mall, the Auburn Mall, and the Aroostook Mall in Presque Isle. While Freeport, with its village of stores, and Kittery, with dozens of outlet shops, are shopping destinations, in most communities smaller stores offering more personal service are the norm.

"I can get most anything I want in town," says Brad Rourke of Camden, "but there's not a great deal of choice. Catalogs help, but they can't supply everything you need."

"Shopping has been my biggest challenge," admits Lynda Chilton of Rockport. "Here in the midcoast we are at least an hours' drive from any mall or large department store. So trips for clothing, shoes, and specialty items which were only fifteen minutes away in Virginia have required some new strategies here. We have had to slow down our expectations, which is not necessarily a bad thing."

New residents have different ways of adapting to the dearth of large department stores. Some take shopping trips to busier areas once in a while. Others rely on catalogs or the Internet for purchases. After all, the growth of catalog and on-line retailing means miles don't matter—you can shop wherever and whenever. (UPS, Federal Express, and Airborne all make regular deliveries, and no extra time is required.) Some folks are pleasantly surprised to find they can live a little more simply in Maine, where consumerism is not a competitive sport. In other words, they buy less.

Of course, not everyone thinks the scarcity of sprawling malls is a hardship. Most people here—newcomers included—far prefer spruces to strip malls, not regretting the absence of the traffic, chain stores, noise, and bustle for which shopping areas have become known. And many come to cherish the kind of personal service smaller shops offer, service that is unavailable in busy big-box retailers. They appreciate the service from booksellers like Maine Coast Books in Damariscotta, for instance, where the owner knows just what type of mystery you enjoy. Or hardware stores like Rankins, in Camden, where second-generation owner Frank Rankin escorts you personally to find the right size of hinge. Service, attention, courtesy, and quality—these are the commonplace little things that make shopping a pleasure in Maine's small stores.

State Spirits

While many of us today are partial to a cup of coffee during the working day, Mainers of the early nineteenth century were far more likely to take "rum breaks." Back then, Maine was a major player in the seagoing "triangle trade" to the West Indies, with "demon rum" a profitable cargo in many a schooner's hold.

Despite (or perhaps because of) this fondness for rum, Maine was the first state to pass laws banning alcoholic beverages, earning it the title, "Birthplace of Prohibition." Temperance may have been popular with some, but others frequented their local bootlegger. More daring were smugglers who made clandestine trips to Canada, rum runners in their sloops, and bands of liquor pirates who raided them.

That exciting era ended with the repeal of Prohibition in the 1930s. Or did it? Some Maine communities rejected the return of legal spirits. To this day the towns of Linneus, Littleton, Monticello, and Blair, all in Aroostook County; Charleston and Corinth, west of Bangor; and the coastal towns of Cushing and Friendship remain "dry."

Outside of these communities, anyone over the age of twenty-one wishing to buy some bubbly can find it readily in Maine at privately owned "agency stores." State-owned establishments are waning as Maine eases out of the liquor market. Maine's agency stores (there are 305) are located within larger supermarkets or convenience stores. Liquor prices are strictly regulated and are higher than in neighboring New Hampshire and Canada, which leads many people to stock up before crossing into Maine. To compete, the state-owned stores in Kittery and Calais offer discount prices—as much as 10 percent lower than in the rest of the state.

No Butts

Unfortunately Maine has a relatively high rate of smoking. With $60 million of its annual Medicaid budget spent on smoking-related illnesses, the state has targeted tobacco use as a high health priority. A 1999 state law bans smoking in all restaurants, although establishments classified as bars are exempt from the law. Smoking is also banned in hospitals and public buildings.

In November 1997 the tax on cigarettes doubled (to $.74 per pack) and a media campaign aimed at discouraging smoking among young Mainers was initiated. Those less than eighteen years of age are prohibited from purchasing tobacco, with stiff fines for vendors who sell to underage smokers.

Although the fight has just begun, these efforts aren't just smoke and mirrors. Since 1998, tobacco consumption in the state has dropped 16 percent, and Governor King has pledged to continue to help Mainers kick the habit.

6 Weather and Wildlife

*"The coldest winter I ever spent was
a summer in Maine."*
—Mark Twain[*]

When talk turns to weather, people who move to Maine year-round are accustomed to incredulous responses from their out-of-state friends. "People in Virginia really freaked us out about winters in Maine," says Lynda Chilton of Rockport. "They acted like we were moving to Siberia!"

The exquisite summers are well known. Maine boasts one of the most comfortable summer climates in the continental United States, a prime reason why thousands of vacationers started "summering" here in the first place. And autumn is nothing short of glorious, with the crimsons and golds of the changing foliage enhanced by sunny, dry days in the sixties and low seventies.

But most of the country harbors exaggerated notions about the severity of Maine's weather come December. Even southern New Englanders believe Old Man Winter saves the full force of his wrath for the Pine Tree State, relentlessly dumping foot after foot of the white stuff on uncomplaining Mainers. And springtime?

"Two words," says transplant Barry Hurtt, a midwesterner now living in Rockland. "Mud season."

A Four-Season Climate

This part of the country has four distinct seasons, and that itself can be a challenge for newcomers accustomed to the same weather no matter what the calendar reads. "I was concerned before moving about dealing with a

----

[*]Mark Twain, quoted in *Portland Monthly* magazine, July 1999.

truly seasonal climate," admits Gary Swanson, who moved with his family to Rockland in 1998. "Coming from California, we've found the weather associated with each of Maine's seasons to be quite dramatic. But if you're prepared, it's really a very livable climate."

There are many good-natured jokes about Maine's seasons, and in particular, their length and arrival dates. People quip that summer hits on the Fourth of July and winter sets in on July 5. Others maintain that "black fly season" comes with the melting snow, and that autumn is announced not by crisp, cool days, but by the onslaught of the fall tourists, or "leaf peepers."

My favorite definition of Maine's meteorological year is that it's "nine months of winter, and three months of mighty rough sleddin'."

MAINE ANNUAL WEATHER FACTS

Precipitation: 43 inches.
Number of thunderstorms: 15 to 20.
Clear days—without fog or other precipitation: 120 days.
Average snowfall on the coast: 50 to 70 inches.
Average snowfall in southern interior section: 60 to 90 inches.
Average snowfall in northern interior section: 90 to 110 inches.
Days with one inch or more snowfall along the coast: 15 to 20 (although a "northeaster" may occasionally drop ten or more inches in a single day).
Days with one inch or more snowfall in the northern interior: 30.
Snowiest month: January, with an average of 20 inches.
Month when hurricanes are most likely to occur: September.
Frequency of tornadoes: rare.
Number of sub-zero days along the coast: 10 to 20.
Number of sub-zero days in the northern interior: 40 to 60.
Peak temperatures: 70° F throughout the state, usually in July, though during a very warm summer, temperatures may reach 90° F for as many as 25 days in the southern interior sections and for as long as a week along the coast.

Freezing temperatures encourage winter activities such as ice skating on smooth lakes and ponds. *Photo courtesy of the Camden Herald.*

But in reality, the climate is generally more moderate (especially along the coast) than in other northern states. Maine's size and its varied topography can make the weather very different in each corner of the state at any given time. Coastal areas receive cool breezes in the summer and warmer air in the winter. When it snows in the western mountains, it may rain Down East and be sunny on the south coast. Kids in Caribou do a great deal more sledding than do their counterparts in Kennebunkport.

WINTER

"Before I moved here, I wondered, 'What are the winters *really* like?'" says Barry Hurtt of Rockland. "But after a decade in Chicago, Maine winters are no big deal."

Anyone accustomed to winters like those dished out in the Midwest can take Maine weather in stride. Contrary to popular belief, winter begins on the late side—some years, not until mid-December. It's generally cold here, ranging between 21 degrees and 32 degrees in January, depending on where you are, but prolonged cold spells of several weeks are rare. Average snowfall ranges from 50 to 110 inches—again, depending on where you are when the flakes fly.

Folks who aren't used to chilly temperatures are often surprised that life goes on even when the mercury drops a little. "We've been amazed to see how active everyone is in the winter," says Thad Chilton of Rockport. "It's great to see families out walking, skiing, and having a good time together." And people who have spent several winters often grow to appreciate the profound beauty of the countryside under a blanket of white and the moody light and colors of the boreal sky.

That's not to say a mean winter can't pack a punch or two, although old-timers claim that today's storms are considerably tamer than the legendary blizzards of yore. The occasional northeaster may drop several inches, prompting television weathermen to put on their sweaters and predict doom and school superintendents to cancel classes. But there is not as much fanfare as you might think. Perhaps because Maine is a state adept at dealing with the white stuff, people often view winter storms more as an occasional treat than a frequent and daunting threat.

"I've been impressed with how well maintained Maine roads are in the winter," notes Allie Lou Richardson of Islesboro. "Crews are at the ready to deal with storms right away."

Elizabeth Burrell of Rockland, a veteran of two Maine winters, agrees. "Don't worry about the weather," she advises. "Towns here are really very well adapted to dealing with whatever comes up."

The ice storm of the twentieth century took place in January 1998. As many as 690,000 Mainers were left without electricity as the weight of a thick coat of ice snapped tree limbs, bringing down power lines all over the Northeast. *Photo courtesy of the* Camden Herald.

Winter around the Country

State	Aver. Temperature (Degrees F)	Aver. Precipitation (Inches)
Connecticut	31.9	13.40
Delaware	39.6	14.08
Maine	19.9	12.17
Maryland	38.0	11.62
Massachusetts	31.1	12.19
New Hampshire	23.8	11.82
New Jersey	35.9	13.56
Pennsylvania	31.0	9.62
Rhode Island	35.0	13.66
Vermont	23.5	10.00
West Virginia	35.3	8.07

SPRING: APRIL IN PARIS (MAINE)

Another time of the year that makes many newcomers pause is the spring, including the interval known fondly in Maine as "mud season."

Unlike some states, Maine is not famous for showy springs. The season that follows winter Down East is a subtle, slow awakening, appreciated more for its quiet clues than boisterous displays. In some years the casual observer has a tough time finding any hint of spring's arrival throughout the chilly gray days of March and April. Because of this, Mainers watch eagerly for signs of the season, noting the first buds on the forsythia and the robin's return. Towns hold annual ice-out contests, with participants guessing when area lakes will become free of winter's grip and open for navigation. Gardeners admire their daffodils, tulips, and jonquils as they break through the warming soil and bloom. And yes, everyone dons mud boots.

SUMMER

If there is one problem with a Maine summer, it's that leaving the state is difficult. Oh, physically, it's easy—the inconveniences that plague other vacation destinations, like crowded roads, high temperatures, or canceled flights are not all that commonplace in Maine, though Route 1 in Wiscasset can become a tangle. Rather, leaving is hard because Maine summers are

March's chilly winds and cool temperatures keep many schooners under wraps until April. *Photo courtesy of the* Camden Herald.

simply extraordinary. With temperatures in the seventies, cool nights, and clean air (the state averaged only one day of unhealthy air in 1999), why would anyone want to leave? More than one Mainer has come back from a summer vacation away and vowed never to depart again. Summers in Maine are a gift—the perfectly green landscape broken only by the colors of gardens, the gentle breezes—even more precious because of their brevity.

AUTUMN

The only thing that makes it bearable to part with summer is the beauty of autumn Down East. September, October, and November are months to treasure. September is often a sunny, crystal-clear month, perfect for hiking, camping, and enjoying the pleasures of summer without the crowds. October ushers in the crispness of fall, along with the glorious colors of the changing foliage. Occasional days of Indian summer can push temperatures into the high seventies, and prompt youngsters to wear shorts to school. November brings the tang of wood smoke to the air, frosted windowpanes, a peaceful landscape, and perhaps a few wispy tufts of snow.

114

GEAR TO GET YOU THROUGH THE SEASONS

Based on a list of tongue-in-cheek suggestions from L.L. Bean's Dave Teufel.

SPRING

- *Bug-proof jacket, pants, and headnet.* These items won't stop the black flies, but will hopefully confuse them long enough for you to make it back from the outhouse.
- *100% pure DEET insect repellent.* You'll need this to keep 'em off you while you're in the outhouse.
- *Traditional "Bean Boots" (the Famous Maine Hunting Shoe with rubber bottom and leather upper).* Height of the uppers depends on where in the state you are moving. In southern Maine, down around Kittery, the ten-inch style is fine, as you only occasionally step in mud. If you plan to spend mud season Down East, in the Lakes Region, or worse, in The County, then you'd best invest in the sixteen-inch version.
- *Rain gear.* Why? Because 50 percent of mud is water.

SUMMER

- You'll want a *canoe or kayak* to get the most out of the summer. But for the love of Pete don't put it off, Maine summers don't last but a few days!
- You'll need a *wetsuit* for going swimming. There's a week, usually late in August, where the ocean temperature soars into the upper 50s. With the right wetsuit, you can usually last a good five minutes before you have to head back to shore.
- A *fly-fishing outfit* is a must. Standing in a cold stream wearing rubber pants was stylish in Maine long before *A River Runs Through It...*
- You'll need a *cooler* to haul all the lobsters you're gonna need when every single flatlander you've ever known shows up at your door for their vacation.

continues →

Many residents, myself included, love autumn best of all. The air is invigorating, and the light takes on a painterly hue that is sometimes breathtaking. It's a beautiful string of russet-colored days, a time of harvest, of thankfulness, and of preparation for the colder weather to come. Tourists have discovered the pleasures of Maine's fall, yet those who come at this

FALL

- Yes, the leaves are beautiful. But it's also mating season for the largest of the hoofed animals; the majestic moose. You will need a *mountain bike* for fast getaways from lovesick bulls on the loose.
- *Running shoes* will come in handy if you find yourself between a moose and a hard place.
- While you're out there, might as well bring your own *tent* and spend a few days camping. The leaf-peepers aren't leaving anytime soon, and there will probably be a few staying at your house.

WINTER

- You'll need *flashlights, candle lanterns, batteries, and camp stoves.* You can count on being out of power for at least four days—unless there is another ice storm like the one in '98, then triple it.
- Sell your fancy car and buy a *truck*. On the way home buy a baseball bat and let the truck have it. (You want to blend in, don't you?) Now, go buy an *auto tow strap, a come-along, and a packable shovel.* The fastest way to the heart of Mainers is to offer them roadside assistance when they are stuck in a snow bank.
- And remember, no matter if you have lived in Maine for sixty years, if you are originally from somewhere else, you will never be considered a Mainer by other Mainers. Just accept it and be proud of your birthplace! Even if you can't get there from here.

time seem more subdued than the boisterous crowds of August. And as each leaf falls, the state grows a little quieter.

"I think the most important thing when considering a move to Maine is to visit in all seasons," says Rockport's Lynda Chilton. "We've found that the weather here is perfect for all kinds of activities year round."

Wildlife

Maine is home to a vast array of wildlife. White-tailed deer, bobcats, black bears, coyote, loons, seals, osprey—the list goes on and on, including threatened species such as bald eagles, Blanding's turtles, and puffins, those colorful "sea parrots" that are making a comeback along the Maine coast. Most famous of all of the state's animals is probably its largest—the moose. "One advantage to moving here," quips Marlene Kinlin of Jonesport, "is watching moose stroll through my front yard."

It isn't every day that a moose comes to call, but living in Maine does make it possible. After all, there are more than thirty-thousand of the big beasts in the state. Their footprints are often visible on muddy hiking trails or dirt roads, and their spreading antlers adorn many a fireplace mantel. Given a little luck and a kayak, you can paddle to a quiet cove on Moosehead Lake and spy one munching aquatic weeds—a favorite treat. On rare occasions, moose will even venture into busy downtown areas or stroll across golf courses.

Rarer by far are sightings of wolves and mountain lions, two recent additions to Maine's endangered species list. Although state biologists have long questioned their existence here, both of these predators are found in Canada, and reports of their presence in Maine persist. In June 2000, a wolflike animal was captured west of Baxter State Park but managed to escape before DNA testing could be done on it. A wolf was trapped in Aurora in 1996, and another one was shot in the Moosehead Lake area in 1993, yet wolf sightings are still extremely rare.

Maine is home to Canada lynx and bobcats, but a verifiable photograph or video of a mountain lion has yet to be taken. Nevertheless, hundreds of reports of cougars are recorded annually with the Department of Inland Fisheries and Wildlife, and several likely tracks have been found. In the

117

Moose often wade into ponds and lakes to munch pondweed and water lily, two nutritious (and apparently delicious) aquatic plants.
Photo by Bill Silliker, Jr., from his book Uses for Mooses *(Down East Books).*

hopes of seeing solid evidence of these secretive felines, wildlife biologists follow up reports in the field and conduct track surveys each winter.

Large predators notwithstanding, it's a relief to discover that Maine lacks many of the poisonous critters that plague other states. There are no poisonous snakes to contend with, no scorpions, and very few venomous insects. Instead, more than one hundred and fifty insects in the order Odonata, damselflies and dragonflies, flit on translucent wings over ponds, bogs, and fields. Nonpoisonous and colorful, they are a significant and conspicuous component of Maine's wildlife diversity.

Stewards of Wildlife

Marlene Kinlin isn't the only Mainer with an affinity for her neighborhood wildlife. Living here often means a closer connection to animals of all types. According to a recent University of Maine study, 53 percent of Maine residents participate in wildlife watching, hunting, or fishing, which ranks the state fourth in the nation after Alaska, Montana, and Idaho. These pastimes also mean tourism dollars for the state. Maine people (including hunters) recognize that wildlife, like any resource, must be responsibly managed, and when necessary, protected.

A good example of this cooperation is the Maine Outdoor Heritage Fund, a partnership between the Sportsman's Alliance of Maine and the Maine

Audubon Society. Created in 1994, the fund is a source of grants for projects that conserve the outdoors for Maine people and wildlife. In what may seem an unlikely alliance—the fishing and hunting crowd and the ardent environmentalists—the two groups started a referendum campaign to establish a lottery ticket dedicated to conservation. So successful were their initial efforts that the legislature implemented the program on its own, bypassing the need for a referendum. Since Maine Outdoor Heritage tickets first went on sale in January, 1996, more than 19 million have been sold, funding over $5.14 million in grants to 185 projects. Tickets are available at most convenience stores, gas stations, and other outlets where Maine State Lottery tickets are sold.

Maine has more than sixty game sanctuaries and wildlife management areas. There are strong laws regulating treatment of wildlife, and wardens and deputy wardens make sure the laws are enforced. Even seemingly innocent acts that endanger wild animals, like the handling of seal pups, are punishable with stiff fines. (Seal pups are born in late spring and are often left on shore while their mothers find food. Never touch a seal pup—instead, call the Marine Animal Lifeline at 207-851-6625 should you find a stray, abandoned, or injured marine mammal.)

Birding

Maine's diversity of coastal and inland habitats offers birders the chance to add lots of feathered friends to their life list—more than 450 species have been identified in the state. Maine is the nesting and breeding ground for numerous migrant species of coastal and inland birds and offers the opportunity to see rare and beautiful species like puffins and loons. In fact, Maine is fortunate to have the largest population of loons in all of New England, estimated at four thousand adults. Since 1977, Maine Audubon Society has been working to protect the common loon in Maine, and thanks to their vigilance, the loon population now seems fairly stable.

For a checklist of Maine birds, contact the Audubon Society at 207-781-2330 or through its website at www.maineaudubon.org. A good reference on where and when to look for particular species is *A Birder's Guide to Maine,* by Liz and Jan Erik Pierson and Peter Vickery (Down East Books, 1996).

Faces from the Past

Currently thirty-four species of fish and wildlife are listed as endangered or threatened under Maine's Endangered Species Act. Some are also listed on the federal government's list.

The state's Department of Inland Fisheries and Wildlife is working with concerned citizens and other groups to boost the dwindling numbers of animals such as piping plovers, box turtles, and twilight moths, and hopefully these efforts will succeed. Some species, like the peregrine falcon, have already shown great progress thanks in large part to protection of nesting sites. (Acadia National Park closes two popular hiking trails during peregrine nesting season.) Other success stories have been the reintroduction of the wild turkey and the Atlantic puffin.

PERSISTENCE PAYS OFF

A common sight (and source of dinner) during colonial days, the wild turkey, North America's largest upland game bird, disappeared from Maine in the early 1800s, largely due to hunting and loss of woodlands. Sportsmen tried reintroducing the birds in 1942, but to no avail. In 1977 and 1978, the Maine Department of Inland Fisheries and Wildlife obtained forty-one wild turkeys from Vermont and released them in the towns of York and Eliot. In spring of 1982, thirty-three turkeys were trapped from the growing York County population and released in Waldo County. Two years later, more birds were relocated, this time to Hancock County, but poaching was believed to be their downfall. During the winters of 1987 and 1988, seventy wild turkeys were obtained from Connecticut to augment Maine's growing population. While some have succumbed to heavy snowfalls, the rest have prospered and multiplied. Today the state's flock has grown to more than eight thousand—so large that hunting the elusive birds is once again allowed.

PUFFIN PATROL

Maine is famous for a multi-colored sea bird, the common or Atlantic puffin. This bird spends most of its time in the North Atlantic, coming ashore only to breed and raise one chick in an underground burrow. A century ago, puffins were found on six Maine islands, but excessive hunting led to their near demise in Maine. By the 1900s, there was only one pair of puffins left

Adult loons on a tranquil lake. Thanks to conservation efforts led by the Maine Audobon Society, loons are a common sight on some waterways. *Photo by Ken Bailey.*

A wild turkey hunts for food in the snow. *Photo by Ernie Rose.*

south of the Canadian border. The lone couple lived on Matinicus Rock, a lonely spot twenty-two miles off the coast in Penobscot Bay. After Matinicus Rock's lighthouse keepers began protecting the puffins from hunters, their numbers began to increase. Today there are about a hundred and fifty nesting pairs on the rock.

In 1973, Stephen Kress, Ph.D., a summer resident of Bremen, began Project Puffin to re-introduce the birds to Eastern Egg Rock in Muscongus Bay. After eight years of trips to Newfoundland to find puffin chicks to "transplant," his efforts, with help from the National Audubon Society, paid off. Today, Maine has puffin colonies on at least four of the original six nesting islands: Eastern Egg Rock, Seal Island, Machias Seal Island, and Matinicus Rock. (The project's website is at www.mainebirding.net/project puffin.)

Several tour boats operate trips to the puffin colonies from different points along the coast in summer. The puffin-watching season begins around

Memorial Day and goes until early to mid-August. For a list of tours, check out www. mainebirding.net or call the Maine Office of Tourism at 207-287-5710.

Moose Watch

Like puffins and turkeys, moose were once in danger of disappearing in Maine. While explorers in the early 1600s found a plentiful supply of moose throughout New England, unrestricted hunting during the centuries that followed decimated the population. By the early 1900s, only two thousand or so moose were left.

Hunting the massive mammals was illegal from 1936 until 1980, and during those years, numbers of the animals slowly grew. In 1979, the moose population had grown so large that a bill allowing the state to issue up to seven hundred hunting permits to Maine resident hunters was signed into law. Since that time, the number of permits issued and the area open to moose hunting has increased. Non-residents are also allowed a percentage of the permits. In 1999, three thousand permits were issued, with five hundred of those earmarked specifically for "antlerless moose." Despite deaths from hunting and highway accidents, the Department of Inland Fisheries and Wildlife estimates that there are approximately thirty-thousand moose in Maine.

MORE THAN YOU EVER THOUGHT YOU'D KNOW ABOUT MAINE MOOSE

- The Latin name for moose, *Alces,* means "elk," and in Europe moose are called elk. The animals are the largest members of the deer family.
- Of the four species of moose found in North America, it's the Eastern Moose that calls Maine home.
- Adult cows (females) weigh around eight hundred pounds. Bulls can weigh more than a thousand pounds.
- The total length of a moose is about nine feet. Height measured at the shoulder is about six feet.
- Both cows and bulls have "bells," or skin flaps on the underside of the neck. A cow's bell looks more like a tuft of hair, whereas a bull's bell is larger and rounder.

122

- The spread of a bull's antlers rarely exceeds sixty-five inches.
- Antlers on cows are extremely rare.
- Moose chomp away on "browse," the leaves and twigs of woody plants. Willow, aspen, birch, maple, pin cherry, and mountain ash are their favorites.
- Balsam fir is a moose's winter junk food: tasty, but nutritionally lacking.
- Aquatic plants, such as pondweed and water lily, are an important part of a moose's diet.
- Moose begin breeding in late September.
- Cows may produce their first calf when they are two. Each May, cows give birth to one or two calves.
- Calves remain with their mother for one year and are driven off shortly before the next calf is born.
- Black bears, which are common in Maine, are potential predators of moose calves.
- The average life expectancy is eight years for a cow and seven years for a bull. Moose may live into their late teens, but rarely live past twenty.
- Moose are found statewide, but most happily thrive in northern Maine.

Deer

According to wildlife biologist Gerry Lavigne, Maine is home to one of the largest subspecies of white-tailed deer, with some mature males, or bucks, weighing nearly four hundred pounds. While approximately 331,000 of these herbivores call Maine home, it's surprising to note that more deer per square mile (fifteen to twenty-five) live in central and southern sections than in the north, where only two to five deer per square mile can be found. In some particularly popular locales to the south, the Department of Inland Fisheries and Wildlife says there are populations of forty to one hundred deer per square mile.

Increasing numbers of deer (and moose, and even turkeys) mean automobile drivers must exercise caution on Maine roads, particularly at dawn and dusk. Take warning signs seriously—in deer or moose zones drive no faster than the speed limit, use your bright lights, and wear your seat belt. Deer tend to travel in groups, so if you spot one, chances are that others are waiting in the woods. And if a deer or moose is standing in the middle of the

A white-tailed deer in winter. Maine's herd is estimated at more than 330,000. *Photo by Ken Bailey.*

road, your best course of action is to slow down, pull over, and exercise patience—honking won't always send them away.

Hunting Season

Avid sportsmen in Maine are in good company—the state has a strong tradition of hunting, fishing, and trapping. Generations of Maine families have hunted in the same quiet spots year after year, or tromped through the spring mud (despite the black flies) to wet a line and fish. Out-of-state hunters and fishermen have headed into the vast woods Down East for more than a century now, staying in remote lodges and employing local guides. Many return to the state each year in search of trophy deer, trout, ducks, or moose.

Fluorescent orange hats, gun racks on pickups, and general stores transformed into tagging stations—all are part of the local scene come fall. Many a new resident has been astonished to meet a camouflaged man with a rifle walking along a woods road, or see a dead deer in a pick-up truck on an autumn afternoon. Whether or not you agree with the practice, hunting is a way of life in Maine. And yes, at times the crack of gunfire echoes through the woods.

Although November is the time of year most associated with hunting, seasons for various animals extend into other times of year as well. Deer season, for example, opens for archers in late September and continues through October. Deer hunting with firearms begins in November and lasts until early December. Hunting is not allowed anywhere in the state on Sunday, but it is always advisable to use caution and wear fluorescent orange outerwear when walking in the woods during hunting season.

For more information on hunting regulations, contact your local town office or city hall, or the Maine Department of Inland Fisheries and Wildlife, at 207-287-8000. Or check out the MDIFW's website at janus.state.me.us/ifw/index.

SAFE HUNTING AND LAND ACCESS

Maine works hard to minimize problems during hunting season. Mike Sawyer, Safety Officer for the Department of Inland Fisheries and Wildlife,

says the state is seeing a definite decrease in hunting accidents, due mainly to safety measures now practiced by many hunters as well as stricter laws and better enforcement. The 1998 hunting season was recorded as one of the safest on record, with only

Entrepreneur and avid hunter Leon Leonwood Bean models his Hunting Safety Coat for an early L.L. Bean catalog. *Photo courtesy L.L. Bean, Inc.*

125

three hunting incidents but no fatalities. "In 1999, we had sixteen incidents, and no fatalities," he notes.

Respect for property is also an important focus. Maine has a long tradition of allowing reasonable access to unposted land. Given that approximately 94 percent of the land in Maine is privately owned, Maine's Inland Fisheries and Wildlife Landowner Relations Program urges hunters to respect landowners' rights to help ensure that access to and use of private property will continue in years to come. Landowners who do not wish hunting on their property may put up signs accordingly, and may orally or in writing tell others to stay off their property. Rules for posting land may be found at http://janus.state.me.us/ifw/hunt/h-post.htm or by calling the MDIFW landowner coordinator at 207-287-8091.

HUNTING LICENSES

Hunting licenses are available for deer, bear, moose, rabbits, bobcats, and foxes as well as a variety of ducks and fowl. To obtain a hunting license for firearms or archery, present a previous year's license (from Maine or

PROFILE

Gordon and Carol Doherty-Cox relocated to Maine after considering a move to the South. "We investigated various areas via the Internet, and we were impressed by the information we found about Maine. We knew where all the banks, theaters, cable companies, and the like were before we even moved," says Carol. "We've found friendly, helpful people here," she says, "and we love the more relaxed lifestyle. However, it's expensive to live here—it's not cheap to drive, heat your house, or cook your food. Variety in shopping is hard to come by, too." Carol and Gordon were surprised by the size of their new state. "We didn't realize how huge Maine is, and we're looking forward to exploring the whole state." The Coxes have some advice for those considering a move to Maine. "Leave your old lifestyle behind, and be prepared to be a part of Maine. If you're looking for a cheaper version of Connecticut, it won't work."

another state) to your local town office, or participating retail store. If you have never hunted, you must present a firearms safety course certificate to the local town office. The certificate is issued after the successful completion of a class on safe hunting given locally once or twice yearly. Archers must also pass a safety course before bow hunting.

You may also meet the requirements to purchase a hunting license on-line through the Department of Inland Fisheries and Wildlife at: https://janus.state.me.us/ifw/moses/licsale.html.

Fishing

Given the abundance and accessibility* of Maine's inland and coastal waterways, the relative simplicity of the gear involved, and the relaxing nature of the sport, it's no wonder fishing is a popular pastime. The images are many: picture a patient fisherman in his ice-fishing shack watching for a "tip-up"; a wader-clad soul casting in a rushing river in late spring; or a group of children jigging for mackerel on a wharf. It's a group of avid anglers around the table at a remote fishing camp, discussing the day's catch while dealing the next poker hand. It's fishing derbies, bait shops, sport-fishing charters, and hatcheries in which millions of trout, slake, and landlocked salmon are raised to stock ponds, lakes, and rivers.

FRESHWATER FISHING

Last year, anglers caught a variety of freshwater species: brook, lake, and brown trout; smallmouth and largemouth bass; white perch, chain pickerel, and landlocked salmon. Licenses are required for people sixteen and older. Most town offices as well as sporting goods stores issue licenses, or they can be ordered on-line from the Inland Fisheries and Wildlife website at: http://janus.state.me.us/ifw/fish/fish.htm, or by mail from: Inland Fisheries and Wildlife, 284 State Street, 41 State House Station, Augusta, ME 04333-0041.

It's sad that Maine lakes, ponds, and rivers have not been spared from polution by mercury. The mercury mostly blows in from out of state and settles into the waters, building up in the bodies of fish. According to the Inland

---

*For more information on both saltwater and freshwater shore access, see page 141.

Fisheries and Wildlife Department, fish that eat other fish show the highest mercury levels, and older fish have more mercury than young fish.

To prevent possible harm from consuming mercury, the Maine Bureau of Health offers the following advice: Pregnant and nursing mothers, women who may get pregnant, and children under eight years of age are advised to limit their intake of fish caught in all Maine inland waters to one meal per month. All other individuals are advised to limit their consumption to one meal per week.

Another health concern relates to water birds rather than humans. "Without a doubt, lead poisoning from lead sinkers and jig heads is the number one killer of adult common loons," says Dr. Mark Pokras, Assistant Professor of Wildlife Medicine at Tufts University School of Veterinary Medicine. Loons, swans, cranes, and other water birds can die a slow and painful death from lead poisoning after swallowing lead fishing sinkers and jigs lost by anglers.

Fish-eating birds can also ingest the lead if a sinker or jig is still attached to the line or to an escaped fish. For the continued health of these birds, don't use equipment that contains lead.

In addition to the Inland Fisheries and Wildlife site, here are two good places for more information: www.fishing-in-maine.com/ and www.flyfishing inmaine.com/.

SALTWATER FISHING

The Department of Marine Resources regulates fishing in coastal waters, where anglers hook a variety of ocean dwellers, including pollack, shad, bluefish, Atlantic cod, haddock, redfish, winter flounder, mackerel, bluefin tuna, and striped bass. While saltwater angling licenses are not required for recreational fishing, it's important to note the strict regulations concerning Atlantic salmon and sturgeon. Basically, it is against the law to "angle, take, or possess" these fish from all Maine waters (including coastal waters). Any Atlantic salmon or sturgeon incidentally caught must be released immediately, alive and uninjured, and at no time should the fish be removed from the water.

Special rules also govern fishing for bluefin tuna and striped bass. For current information, contact the Recreational Marine Fisheries Program, Maine Department of Marine Resources, P.O. Box 8, West Boothbay Harbor,

ME 04575. Telephone: 207-633-9500. Specifics on size limitations, red tide contamination of shellfish, and other saltwater topics are available on their website at http://janus.state.me.us/dmr/recreational/homepage.html, as well as at http://janus.state.me.us/ifw/fish/f-salt.htm.

As in other parts of the country, many fishermen today free their fish in an effort to promote healthy stocks. For tips on catch and release techniques, try this site: www.destinationmaine.com/fishing/bruce/catchrel.htm.

Harvesting Shellfish

Wondering whether you can dig your own clams or pick a bushel of mussels for dinner? Although the state allows anyone to dig up to a half bushel of clams without a license, most coastal communities have ordinances requiring some type of permit, so check with your town office before planning your clambake. Lobsters require a recreational license from the state, which allows use of up to five traps. Snails, whelks, and scallops all require a license as well. (See the Department of Marine Resources website for particulars: www.state.me.us/dmr, or call them at 207-633-9500.)

Anyone can pick up to two bushels of mussels without a mussel license; however, when harvesting any seafood, it's wise to check and make sure an area isn't closed due to pollution or red tide. The DMR's shellfish sanitation hotline is constantly updated and can be reached at 800-232-4733.

Wildlife Health Issues

RABIES

Most people find wildlife watching a rewarding experience. The thrill of spotting a deer, seeing a red-tailed hawk in flight, or glimpsing a porcupine as it shuffles off into the underbrush, never seems to diminish. While observing wild animals from a distance is perfectly fine, feeding or petting them is never wise, particularly because of the threat of rabies, a dangerous and lethal disease.

Rabies is a virus that can infect any mammal. In 1997, there were 244 clinically confirmed cases of rabid animals in Maine. The southern counties had the highest share, although the disease is slowly creeping northward. The Maine Department of Inland Fisheries and Wildlife says that some animals—raccoons, skunks, woodchucks, and foxes—are particularly susceptible to the disease. The department notes that bats are also high-risk carriers, but rodents such as squirrels, rats, mice, and chipmunks very rarely have the disease. (In fact, you should always use extreme caution with bats, alive or dead.)

Thanks to vaccines, rabies is extremely rare among pets and farm animals. How can you tell if a wild animal is rabid? Diseased animals usually behave abnormally, but experts say signs can vary. Some rabid animals appear shy and fearful, while others become aggressive. Still others may simply stumble as though drunk or appear lame. If you believe an animal may be rabid, contact your town's animal control officer. Suspected animals who have come in contact with either a human or domestic animal are tested by the Health and Environmental Testing Laboratory in Augusta.

MAINE'S FAMOUS FLIES

Some Mainers jokingly refer to black flies as the "state bird." The pesky insects are one of four particularly annoying pests in Maine, the other three being mosquitoes, large biting flies (deer, horse, and moose flies) and no-see-ums, or midges. Of these the black fly probably wins the award for most irritating.

As anyone who has attempted a stroll through the woods in late May knows, black flies are at their hungriest in the spring. Their season lasts roughly from mid-May until the end of June, or as people like to say, "from Mother's Day to Father's Day." The bite of the black fly is tiny, but vicious, causing open wounds and, in some people, noticeable swelling. Mainers cope with the arrival of black flies in sensible ways, wearing light-colored clothing, long sleeves, and a little repellent. Breezes help, too, and early morning is often the best time to be outdoors during black fly season. But take heart: anecdotal evidence suggests that newcomers to black fly territory react most severely to the bites. After a couple of years many people find that their bodies do seem to adjust, and the bites are not so painful and itchy.

Mosquitoes and the larger biting flies can be kept at bay through the use of repellents. Not so for the tiny midges known as no-see-ums. They are most active at dusk and are unfazed by clothing color or most repellents. Their bite is like a tiny pinprick, irritating but not as severe as a black fly's.

One annoying characteristic of this tiny creature: its small size means it can sneak through many window screens.

TICKS

You'll rarely be bothered by the large, clinging American dog tick in Maine, but you may encounter the tiny deer tick, which, unlike its bigger cousins, does not stay attached to its victim. Were it not for the threat of Lyme disease, deer ticks would simply be bothersome insects. But Lyme disease is a serious condition, causing flu-like symptoms and, in severe cases, arthritis and damage to the nervous system and heart. Spread through the bite of a deer tick, Lyme disease is becoming more prevalent in Maine, particularly in the southern counties, although it is still considerably less common here than in states to the south.

It is too soon to know whether a new vaccine, recently approved by the federal Food and Drug Administration, will stop the spread of the disease. Researchers say the vaccine is 80 percent effective and requires three shots over a year. So far, it has not been approved for children under fifteen.

Another development may stop the spread of Lyme disease in the future by killing ticks on the deer themselves. A recent invention by researchers at the University of Rhode Island sprays a natural fungus at a deer's head, eliminating ticks without harming the host animal.

Without proven solutions, some island communities—most notably Monhegan and Peaks Island—have had to make tough decisions on whether to exterminate their rapidly growing deer populations in order to prevent the disease's spread. In both cases, islanders voted by a narrow margin to eliminate deer herds.

To prevent bites from ticks, wear hats, pants, and long-sleeved clothing when walking or hiking in the woods or fields. Use repellent and check yourself and your children or pets when you head in from the outdoors. If a deer tick bites you, check with your doctor for the signs of Lyme disease, which is treatable, especially when caught early.

7 Vacationland

"When you live in Maine you know that you're going to be bitten by black flies, annoyed by tourists and, come fall, disappointed by the Red Sox."

— John McDonald*

Maine's tourism industry began in the period following the Civil War. "Sports" from the Northeast were lured to the North Woods by tales of game and adventure, wealthy families were attracted by cool coastal breezes. Railroad tracks for Maine Central crisscrossed the state, and steamships from Boston and ports south docked several times daily at coastal wharves. It wasn't long before impressive Victorian resorts began to spring up along the coast, as well as inland on large lakes like Moosehead and Sebago. Soon business was booming. Restaurants served lobster thermidor, yacht clubs held regattas, and dancing pavilions hosted orchestras that played to throngs of summer visitors.

From the beginning, Maine was a haven both for the moneyed and the masses. Summer colonies like those in Bar Harbor, Islesboro, and York Harbor attracted presidents, socialites, and the scions of America's wealthiest families, while nearby honky-tonk beach towns were frequented by working-class families who frolicked in the chilly surf. Religious groups held summer-long revivals here, the tang of the sea air lending a salty counterpoint to the sermons. For tourists then, as now, Maine represented clean air, relaxation, recreation, and nature.

Not all of the state is a tourist mecca, but chances are, even the sleepiest of towns benefit from the state's popularity in some shape or form. Tax revenues, for instance. In 1998, $299.3 million was brought in through taxes paid by tourists. Tourism is generally seen as a clean, nonpolluting

----

*John McDonald, October 18, 1999, article on his website at http://story tellers.maine.com

industry. And tourism allows many residents the independence of owning their own businesses.

What is it like to live in Vacationland? By far, the best benefit is the ability to enjoy year-round what others try to squeeze in during a brief few days. Fishing, hiking, sailing, skiing—the list is practically endless. Living in Maine means taking full advantage of the nearly limitless possibilities this great state provides.

Memories of Maine

Indeed, many new residents were once tourists or summer people. David Njaa, who relocated to Belfast from Chicago, has fond memories of the family cottage (Mainers tend to call them camps) on a small pond in Lincolnville. Marlene Kinlin and her husband, Sarge, moved to the state after years

PROFILE

Marlene Kinlin and her husband, Sarge, moved up from Wrentham, Massachusetts, in 1994 after building a retirement home on a point in Jonesport. The couple had always loved coastal Maine, and were attracted to Washington County by the breathtaking yet affordable property for sale. "I wondered whether I would become a part of the Jonesport community," says Marlene. "But I've met fascinating women through my book club, and I have wonderful, helpful neighbors." She drew on the strength of those friendships when Sarge unexpectedly died in 1995. "I would never have guessed I would stay here alone," she admits. "Sometimes I feel isolated, but I think that's my problem, not Maine's."

Like many folks who live in Vacationland, she hosts friends and family quite often during the warm months. "It's such a pleasure to entertain guests here," she says. "They can't help but love the incredible views." To those considering relocation in the state, Marlene Kinlin offers this advice: "Be sure you have inner resources. Maine will welcome you if you have strength of character. I'm still working on it."

of family vacations on Damariscotta Lake. Thad Chilton of Rockport had vacationed only briefly in Maine, but had a feeling his wife would love it here.

"We like the mountains and skiing," Chilton explains. "We enjoy boating, swimming, and fishing. We like wide-open spaces, and small towns where you're not anonymous. I knew Lynda would love Maine, and sure enough, on her first trip here she was collecting real estate brochures."

Between the lighthouses, loons, schooner trips, and skiing trails, the hardest part of living in Maine is often deciding which activities to pursue. Despite the state's reputation for a slow pace of life, Mainers can be as busy as they want to be. The sites and activities described below are just a few of the many possibilities.

If you'd like even more options, two Maine tourism associations offer a wealth of ideas: The Maine Office of Tourism, the state's official tourism authority located in Augusta, www.visitmaine.com, and the Maine Tourism Association, a Hallowell-based organization formerly called the Maine Publicity Bureau, 207-623-0363; www.mainetourism.com. (For additional information on museums, refer to chapters 8 and 9.)

Hiking

The undulating landscape provides hikers with some of the best trekking terrain in the country, from relatively easy jaunts through nature preserves to more challenging climbs up steep mountains where unparalleled vistas await. Great hikes can be found in every corner in Maine—out almost everyone's back door. In addition, there are four world-class trail systems:

- *Acadia National Park.* Trails and carriage roads in Maine's only national park take day hikers up over coastal mountains, offering remarkable prospects of sea and shore. Acadia National Park, P.O. Box 177, Bar Harbor, ME 04609. 207-288-3338. www.nps.gov/acad/home.htm.
- *Appalachian Trail.* The famous hiking highway runs 276 miles through Maine, from the New Hampshire border to the AT's northern terminus at Mount Katahdin. Many who have hiked the whole trail call Maine's section the most beautiful. For information contact the Maine Appalachian Trail Club, P.O. Box 283, Augusta, ME 04332-0283. www.nps.gov.

▲*Baxter State Park.* Home of Mount Katahdin, the "forever wild" back-country park has more than fifty interconnecting trails that ramble for hundreds of miles, across peaks and to remote ponds. Some of the most beautiful scenery in Maine can be found within the bounds of the park. Reservations (required for overnight stays) are limited and in great demand. Contact Baxter State Park, 64 Balsam Drive, Millinocket, ME 04462. 207-723-5140. www.gorp.com/gorp/resource/statepark/ me_baxte.htm.

▲*White Mountain National Forest.* Many are surprised to learn that close to fifty-thousand acres of this national forest, normally associated with New Hampshire, are located along Maine's western border, allowing access to more than two hundred interconnecting trails.

For information on hikes in your area, contact your local chamber of commerce, the indispensable DeLorme *Maine Atlas and Gazetteer,* the Appalachian Mountain Club's excellent *Maine Mountain Guide,* or give the Maine Outdoor Adventure Club a call at 207-879-7490.

THE TEN HIGHEST PEAKS IN MAINE

Name	County	Height above sea level	Relative Climb above base
Katahdin	Piscataquis	5,267	4,674
Sugarloaf	Franklin	4,237	2,931
Old Speck	Oxford	4,180	2,690
Crocker	Franklin	4,168	2,949
Bigelow	Somerset	4,150	3,028
North Brother	Piscataquis	4,143	1,323
Saddleback	Franklin	4,116	2,596
Abraham	Franklin	4,049	2,809
The Horn	Franklin	4,023	2,923
Spaulding	Franklin	3,988	2,748

In Baxter State Park, the Knife Edge is a hair-raising trail that traverses outcrops and boulders to connect Mount Katahdin's Chimney Peak to Baxter Peak. *Photo by Susan Trenholm.*

State Parks

Maine is home to more than thirty state parks, which are enjoyed by residents all year long. Twelve state parks and the Allagash Wilderness Waterway provide camping, and a number of sites require reservations. For more information about the reservation system, call 800-332-1501, or see the Bureau of Parks and Lands website at www.state.me.us/doc/parks.htm.

In addition to camping, state parks provide the dramatic backdrop for a range of day-use activities, from picnicking to ocean swimming. Here's a sampling, including some of the lesser-known gems.

- *Aroostook State Park.* On Echo Lake south of Presque Isle, this 577-acre park offers hiking on 1,213-foot Quaggy Joe Mountain and trout fishing on Echo Lake, as well as campsites, a bathhouse, and a beach with a lifeguard. Groomed cross-country ski trails are available when the snow flies. 207-768-8341.

- *Damariscotta Lake State Park.* A family favorite in Jefferson, this lakeside park is known for its sand beach, patrolled by lifeguards. It's also a popular place for picnics on summer evenings, with its group shelter and grills. 207-549-7600.

- *Grafton Notch State Park.* Some of Maine's better hiking crisscrosses this mountainous park north of Bethel—several trails extend through the Mahoosuc Range. But you don't have to be a trekker to enjoy the

state park here. It also features several stunning roadside gorges.
207-824-2912.

▲ *Moose Point State Park.* On Route 1 between Belfast and Searsport,
Moose Point is one of Maine's smaller and lesser-known state parks.
Those in the know enjoy its picnic facilities, short but fun hiking trail,
and exceptional views of Penobscot Bay. 207-548-2882.

▲ *Peaks–Kenney State Park.* Another of the state's less-busy parks, this
beauty sits on lovely Sebec Lake just north of the picturesque community of Dover-Foxcroft. There's a swimming beach, camping facilities,
and great upcountry vistas. 207-564-2003.

▲ *Roque Bluffs State Park.* Just south of Jonesboro, this Down East area
has one of the few pebble beaches in Maine as well as a freshwater
pond. Hardy swimmers take to the waters here and picnickers enjoy
the ocean breezes. 207-255-3475.

▲ *Swan Lake State Park.* North of Swanville, Maine's newest state park
provides swimming and a playground. 207-525-4404.

▲ *Wolfe's Neck Woods State Park.* What makes this park unique is its
proximity to bustling downtown Freeport. Only 4.5 miles from L.L.
Bean, Wolfe's Neck sits on more than two hundred acres and offers
guided trails, picnic tables, and views of Casco Bay and the Harraseeket River. 207-865-4465.

On the Waters

SEA KAYAKING

Virtually everyone who tries this growing sport seems to become a fan.
"Want to see how popular sea kayaking has become in Maine?" one outfitter
asks. "Stand on the side of the Maine Turnpike in summer and count the
skinny boats on the tops of cars." Indeed, the sport has exploded in the past
decade, and Maine—with more than 3,500 miles of coast, as many islands,
and innumerable bays and coves—is a paddler's paradise. Quite aside from
the state's renowned natural beauty, it's also home to the Maine Island Trail,
a network of islands along the length of the coast open to conscientious
visitors. (Maine Island Trail Association, P.O. Box C, Rockland, ME 04841,
207-596-6456, www.mita.org.)

Sea kayaking tours are a popular way to discover the quiet coves and inlets of the coast. *Photo courtesy of the* Camden Herald.

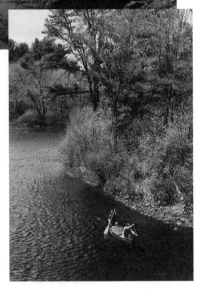

Canoeing the Saco and Great Ossipee Rivers in Cornish. *Photo by Ernie Rose.*

There are outfitters from Kittery to Calais now offering sales, rentals, and guided half-day and full-day trips, including equipment to keep you safe and dry. After a short clinic, you'll be ready to paddle off on a coastal adventure. The Office of Tourism site has loads of sea kayaking information. The site is www.visitmaine.com.

CANOEING

As Maine Guides and the natives before them knew, canoes are the perfect vessel for exploring lakes and ponds, allowing paddlers to get right up close and personal to the water. Maine's premier canoe company, Old Town, has an interesting web site offering information on the heritage of the Maine canoe plus loads of links to other sites—www.oldtowncanoe.com. One of the state's most popular canoeing destinations is the Allagash River Waterway, a world-famous chain of lakes and rivers stretching for close to one hundred miles in the northern part of Maine. The state has a wealth of canoe outfitters ready to send you paddling downriver or across a tranquil pond. Check out www.visitmaine.com for more ideas.

TEN LARGEST LAKES IN MAINE

Maine is dotted with more than twenty-five hundred lakes and ponds. Not all allow boats or personal watercraft, so check first with local authorities or the area chamber of commerce. Here are Maine's very biggest bodies of fresh water.

Name	Town	Square Miles
Moosehead	Little Squaw Township	117.02
Sebago	Sebago	44.95
Chesuncook	T3 R12 WELS	36.05
Flagstaff	Flagstaff Township	31.72
Pemadumcook	T1 R10 WELS	28.59
Spednic	Vanceboro	26.90
Mooselookmeguntic	Richardson Township	25.47
Grand Lake (east)	Forest City Township	25.11
Grand Lake (west)	T5 ND BPP	22.41
Chamberlain	T7 R12 WELS	17.32

WHITEWATER RAFTING

Northern Maine offers exciting Class III to Class V whitewater from early May to early October on the Kennebec, Penobscot, and Dead Rivers. Because of controlled dam releases from hydroelectric plants, Maine is the only state in the Northeast that can guarantee high water, along with unmatched scenery and wildlife. Two rivers, the Kennebec and the Dead, converge at The Forks, headquarters for most of Maine's rafting companies.

SHORELAND ACCESS

Most of Maine's shoreland, whether bordering the ocean or lakes and ponds, is privately owned. Until recently, the whole question of ownership was treated informally, with few proprietors caring if their stretch of beach was strolled upon. Thankfully, this attitude still prevails in some places, but in other spots, shorefront is posted to keep beachcombers off.

While many newcomers assume they can legally walk private shoreland below the high-tide line, unfortunately that's not the case. Maine's laws regarding shoreland access derive from the Colonial ordinance of 1642, which states that property owners own to the low-water mark. While the ordinance provides that others may use the flats (the land between the high- and low-water marks) for "navigation, fishing, or fowling," that does not include strolling or picnicking or swimming.

Many coastal towns maintain a town wharf or public boat launching site. A tremendous benefit for Maine residents is the state's network of public shore-access sites. Marked on the De-Lorme atlas as well as other maps, these areas provide everyone a way to get out on the water. Some, though not all, have vehicle-accessible boat ramps and parking space for cars.

The West Branch of the Penobscot, largest of the three rivers, flows a few miles from towering Mt. Katahdin. For more information, call Raft Maine at 207-824-3694 or see their site at www.raftmaine.com.

SAILING

Some yachters have claimed that island-studded Penobscot Bay offers the best sailing this side of the Mediterranean. And that's only the start. For literally hundreds of years, the state's thirty-seven hundred miles of seacoast have been considered a sailor's dream. Deep harbors, quiet coves, good anchorages, and thousands of islands add up to memorable cruising trips, whether your vessel is a twenty-eight-foot sloop or fifty-foot yacht. If you don't (yet) own a boat, take a two-hour day sail on an historic vessel or spend several days aboard a Maine Windjammer. You'll quickly see why many believe Maine offers the very best sailing in the world. (Maine Windjammer Association, P.O. Box 1144, Blue Hill, ME 04614. 207-374-2993. www.sailmainecoast.com.)

In the Snow

CROSS-COUNTRY SKIING

No matter where you live in Maine, once the snowflakes fall you're not far from a place to cross-country ski. This winter sport has been part of Maine's heritage since 1870. Some say it was even introduced to the U.S. here, when the Swedish immigrants who founded the Aroostook County village of New Sweden brought with them their traditional ten-foot wooden skis with leather bindings. Today's Nordic skiers have more sophisticated equipment, but they enjoy the same beautiful countryside as did those early enthusiasts.

The state has several fancy cross-country ski centers where groomed trails and virtually unlimited backcountry skiing await. Favorite sites are Acadia National Park in Bar Harbor and the Bethel Inn Ski Touring Center in Bethel. The Maine Nordic Ski Council, 800-754-9263 or www.mnsc.com, has more information.

SNOWMOBILING

Thousands of miles of signed, groomed snowmobile trails interconnect across Maine like mini-highways, circling frozen lakes, winding through snow-capped spruces, and meandering along country roads. Festivals, poker runs, organized rides, hill climbs, and radar runs keep scores of sledders and snowmobile clubs busy throughout the colder months. For more information on trails, you can contact the Maine Snowmobiling Association at 800-880-7669, or see their web site at www.mesnow.com.

ALPINE SKIING AND SNOWBOARDING

"Maine is blessed with a wide variety of ski areas," says Greg Sweetser, Executive Director of the Ski Maine Association. "We've got everything from world-class resorts like Sunday River and Sugarloaf to classic community areas like the Camden Snow Bowl, where you can see the ocean from the top of Ragged Mountain. There are underdeveloped big mountains with un-

A snowboarder catches some air at Sugarloaf USA in Carrabasset Valley. Snowboarding has taken off at mountains everywhere, and Maine's slopes offer winter parks as well as challenging natural terrain. *Photo by Victoria Doudera.*

matched scenery, like Saddleback and Big Squaw, and everything in between."

If you enjoy downhill skiing or snowboarding, a clear advantage to living in the state is proximity to the slopes. From Lonesome Pine Trails in Fort Kent to Shawnee Peak in Bridgton (northern New England's largest night-skiing mountain) most Mainers live within an easy drive of short lift lines, superior snow, and uncrowded trails. And unlike slopes in the west, several of Maine's ski areas are alongside beautiful lakes, making for more activities available year round. "There are a variety of programs for all ages, too," adds Greg Sweetser. "Race leagues, learn-to-ski or -board clinics, women's programs—you name it."

Youngsters in Maine have the opportunity to learn downhill sports at an early age. "Many communities have really strong programs in place where kids four to twelve learn how to ski," notes Sweetser. "Even Portland and Bangor, which you wouldn't think of as ski towns, have school programs." The Maine Ski Association also sponsors the Fifth Grade Ski Pass, in which every fifth-grader in the state can enjoy free skiing and snowboarding at many Maine mountains.

For a complete list of ski areas, call the Maine Ski Association at 207-761-3774, or visit their website at www.skimaine.com.

Outdoor Education

Whether you want to learn to tie your own flies or master the J-stroke, a course at one of Maine's outdoor-education schools can show you the ropes. Take up a new sport, perfect one you already enjoy, or become a knowledgeable Registered Maine Guide. Outdoor courses are a great way to get to know Maine and Mainers fast.

- ▲ *Kittery Trading Post*, Kittery. Maine's second-most-famous outfitter offers instruction in kayaking, fly-fishing, fly-tying, and hunting. Call 207-439-2700 ext. 240 or 888-KTP-MAINE for more information.

- ▲ *L.L. Bean Outdoor Discovery Program*, Freeport. The sporting-goods giant provides a wealth of resources and instruction year-round in everything from wingshooting to bicycling. Call 800-341-4341, ext. 6666 for more information.

- ▲ *Maine Sport Outdoor School*, Rockport. Known for its kayaking courses and trips, Maine Sport also offers courses in becoming a Registered Maine Guide and wilderness medicine. Call 207-236-8797 for more info.

- ▲ *Maine Bound*, Orono. An amazing resource based at the University of Maine, Maine Bound grew from an outing club to an outfitter to a provider of instruction. Rent everything from canoes to crampons at reasonable prices, sign up for a mountaineering course, or head out on a ice-climbing expedition. Call 207-581-1794 for more information.

- ▲ *Maine Audubon Society*, Falmouth. From its nature centers in Falmouth and Holden (outside of Bangor), Maine Audubon offers a host of field trips and classes in subjects from bird watching to plant identification. Very reasonably priced, these seminars will help you quickly get to know your way around your Maine backyard. Call 207-781-2330 for more information.

- ▲ *The Nature Conservancy*, Brunswick. Workshops and outings have become a regular offering of this well-known conservation organization. See rare species up close or canoe a newly saved river. Call 207-729-5181 for details.

Lighthouses

Maine is justifiably famous for its lighthouses. Here's a partial list, beginning in York and proceeding Down East along the coast. Included are only those beacons where close-up views are possible. For a complete list, contact the Maine Tourism Association at www.mainetourism.com.

144

Portland Head Light, one of Maine's best-known lighthouses. *Photo by Ted Panayotoff.*

⚓ *Cape Neddick,* York. A forty-one-foot white cast-iron conical tower, on the summit of Cape Neddick Nubble, this coastal sentinel was built in 1879.

⚓ *Spring Point Ledge,* South Portland. A white brick and cast-iron cylindrical tower, the light at Spring Point illuminates the west side of the main channel of Portland Harbor. It was built in 1897.

⚓ *Portland Head Light,* Cape Elizabeth. Maine's most famous and most recognizable light, this eighty-foot white fieldstone and brick tower was built in 1791 under the authorization of George Washington.

⚓ *Pemaquid Light,* Pemaquid Point. The Pemaquid peninsula's thirty-two-foot, conical fieldstone tower was built in 1827 and is a popular place to watch crashing surf.

⚓ *Monhegan Light,* Monhegan Island. Atop the enchanting midcoast island, the Monhegan Light was constructed in 1824 and looks out across Monhegan harbor and nearby Manana Island.

⚓ *Marshall Point Light,* Port Clyde (St. George). A twenty-five-foot white granite tower with an oft-photographed footbridge, Marshall Point light was erected in 1832.

- ⚲ *Rockland Breakwater Light,* Rockland. While it's a small lighthouse by Maine standards, the eighteen-foot square tower atop the Rockland Breakwater's fog signal house is among the most fun to visit because it sits at the end of a mile-long stone breakwater that juts clear into the middle of the harbor.
- ⚲ *Owls Head Light,* Owls Head. Built in 1825, this is a twenty-foot white conical tower, constructed of brick.
- ⚲ *Grindel Point Light,* Islesboro. Accessible by car ferry from Lincolnville. This tall island sentinel was built in 1851.
- ⚲ *Bass Harbor Head Light,* Bass Harbor. Built in 1858, this twenty-six-foot cylindrical tower sits on a ledge on Mount Desert Island's "quiet side," and attracts some spillover tourist traffic from Acadia National Park.
- ⚲ *West Quoddy Head Light,* Lubec. Set dramatically above soaring cliffs at the easternmost Maine point and looking out at the Bay of Fundy, this forty-nine-foot tower is the state's only red-and-white painted light. Great hiking trails wander along the shore and through the woods of the surrounding state park.

Covered Bridges

Once there were 120 covered bridges in the state of Maine, but most were lost to fire, flood, ice, and "progress." Here's a list of nine covered bridges, and the rivers they cross, from the Maine Office of Tourism. If you'd like more information, consult the Department of Transportation's website at: www.state.me.us/mdot/maint_op/covered/splash.htm.

- ⚲ *Babb's Bridge.* Crossing the Presumpscot River, Babb's is Maine's oldest covered bridge, built in 1843. It is located off the River Road, between the towns of Gorham and Windham. Burned in 1973, it has since been rebuilt.
- ⚲ *Hemlock Bridge.* Located off Route 302 in the town of Fryeburg, this old bridge spans a channel of the Saco River. Built in 1857, it is of Paddleford truss construction with supporting laminated wooden arches.
- ⚲ *Low's Bridge.* Originally built in 1857, carried away when the

Piscataquis River flooded in 1987, and rebuilt in 1990, this structure connects the upcountry villages of Sangerville and Guilford.

⚑ *Sunday River Bridge.* Also known as "the Artists' Bridge," this span is the most painted and photographed bridge in the state. It was built in 1872 in Newry.

⚑ *Porter Bridge.* Constructed as a joint project by the towns of Porter and Parsonsfield, Porter Bridge is a unique two-span structure, put in place above the Ossipee River in 1876.

⚑ *Robyville Bridge.* Situated above Kenduskeag Stream, this Corinth span is the only completely shingled covered bridge in Maine.

⚑ *Lovejoy Bridge.* At only seventy feet long, Lovejoy Bridge is the shortest covered bridge in Maine. It's perched above the Ellis River in the town of Andover.

⚑ *Bennet Bridge.* Spanning the Magalloway River in Lincoln Plantation, this relatively young bridge was built in 1901.

⚑ *Watson Settlement Bridge.* In the town of Littleton, the Watson Settlement Bridge has two distinctions: it is the newest covered bridge—built in 1911—and also the farthest north in Maine.

Exploring Waters and Sky

⚑ *Bar Harbor Oceanarium* (207-288-5005). This museum features a harbor seal exhibit, lobster museum, and salt marsh trails.

⚑ *Southwest Harbor Oceanarium* (207-244-7330). More than twenty tanks containing Maine sea life are located here.

⚑ *Harbor Aquarium* (Boothbay Harbor, 207-633-9542). Coastal sea life is on display.

⚑ *Maine Marine Fisheries Aquarium* (Boothbay, 207-633-5572). This new facility features displays of regional fish.

⚑ *Craig Brook Fish Hatchery* (Orland, 207-469-2803). Open seasonally.

⚑ *Bar Harbor Whale Museum* (Bar Harbor, 207-288-2339). Maine's gentle giants of the deep are celebrated here.

⚑ *University of Maine Planetarium* (Orono, 207-581-1341). This newly remodeled star-gazing facility is on the second floor of Wingate Hall.

Golf

Mainers love their links, and the state offers close to forty eighteen-hole courses and more than sixty nine-hole courses scattered across the landscape. Many are challenging; virtually all are breathtakingly beautiful. Two are considered premier courses: Rockport's Samoset Golf Club, known as the "Pebble Beach of the East," and the Sugarloaf Golf Club located in Carrabassett Valley. A third course, the Belgrade Lakes Golf Club, was recently rated the fifth best "New Upscale" course in the country by *Golf Digest* magazine.

Portland is home to the Maine Golf Hall of Fame (P.O. Box 8142, Portland ME 04104-8142. Phone 207-799-0983.)

For a complete list of courses in Maine, try this website: www.travel golfmaine.com, or pick up a copy of *The Guide to Maine Golf Courses,* by Park Morrison (Down East Books, 2000).

Professional Sports Teams

In addition to NCAA champion university and college squads, Maine has two professional sports teams. Both are located in Portland.

- *Portland Sea Dogs.* A trip to cheer on Portland's minor league AA baseball team at Hadlock Field is fun for the whole family. The Sea Dogs are an affiliate of the Florida Marlins and have fast become Portland's hometown team. Seats are close enough to see all the action, tickets are cheap, and the players play for the love of the game. Call 207-879-9500 for information, or see the team's website at www.portlandseadogs.com.

- *Portland Pirates.* Exciting American League Hockey is played at the Cumberland County Civic Center each winter, where the crowd cheers on the swashbuckling Pirates. Call 207-828-4665 for information, or check the club's website at www.portlandpirates.com.

Higher Education and Cultural Life

"Maine is least appreciated of the fifty states."
—ANDY ROONEY*

For centuries, Maine has been an inspiration for artists, musicians, and writers, yet one of the biggest fears of new residents is that a move to Maine means exile from the world of culture. "I questioned whether I could put myself in a rural situation and not miss the culture and hubbub of Boston," says Dottie Paradis of Cornish.

Brad Rourke and his wife Andrea Jarrell shared this same anxiety: "Our big concern was how rural Maine is," says Brad. "We were worried that we would become restless and bored without the stimulation of a major city."

The longing for the bright lights of a big city has prompted these and many other new Mainers to take frequent pilgrimages back to the bustle. "I travel far and wide for cultural stimulation," says Dottie Paradis. "It's a lot of miles, but one trip to Portland will last me about a week. I travel to Boston about once a month."

Clearly, a rural or small-town lifetyle does not have all of the cultural perks of urban living; nor, of course, does it have the problems of urban living. But the question remains: Is culture lacking in the Pine Tree State, or is it a question of perception?

"We're happy and pleased that we made the move to Maine," says Carol Doherty-Cox of Port Clyde. "We investigated various areas on the Internet and were impressed with the information we found on the midcoast area in particular. But we've heard stories from others who've had difficulty adjusting to the lack of shopping or their (perceived) cultural isolation."

---

*Andy Rooney, speaking at the Gray-New Gloucester High School commencement, June 11, 2000.

Most newcomers are pleasantly surprised to discover that Maine has much more to offer than lighthouses and loons. In fact, the state boasts a wealth of cultural and educational activities to keep most people happily enriched—museums of all kinds, theater in all settings, music of all varieties, and scores of festivals, workshops, and classes.

Some new residents find their new, less stressful lifestyles give them leave to participate in or try activities they couldn't find time for before. "I've started studying piano since we moved to Maine," says Lynda Chilton. "With my hectic lifestyle in Virginia, that just wasn't an option."

"For me, the biggest advantage to living in Maine is the small-town feeling with big city availability," says Barry Hurtt of Rockland. "From wonderful little book stores, to Maine PBS, to the variety of arts and music—there is actually *too much* available."

What also surprises new residents is the quality of activities available away from the state's larger cities. "There are excellent concerts and theater programs in Down East Maine," says Marlene Kinlin of Jonesport. "And I've audited courses at the University of Maine in Machias that were terrific."

PROFILE

Mary Griffin relocated to the Bangor region from Charleston, South Carolina, in 1996 so her husband could attend graduate school at the University of Maine. "I was concerned about the move," she admits. "I'd only been to Maine once, and that was a day trip to L.L. Bean from Cape Cod." Griffin's biggest worry was whether she'd find a decent job. "I landed one of the most challenging and rewarding positions I've ever had. I love Bangor, and the people are just fantastic."

Now that her husband has earned his M.B.A., Griffin hopes they will remain in Maine. "We're having a difficult time finding a job that will justify his degree," she explains. "Unfortunately, we may have to look at other states or regions, but we eventually will come back. It's definitely the best thing we've ever done. I would wholeheartedly, unreservedly, recommend a move to Maine. It truly is 'The way life should be.'"

Only in Maine can you learn to build a Friendship sloop, hear a Bach cantata performed by the country's oldest symphony orchestra, and rub elbows with the founder of a multinational computer company at a cutting-edge technological conference. Maine offers its residents diverse opportunities that aren't usually found in a rural state: the chance to study Russian with a native, for example, or play the harp at a world-renowned harp colony, or take in an exhibit of Andrew Wyeth's paintings in a highly regarded museum not far from where they were painted.

You can tour a Shaker village, visit Revolutionary War General Henry Knox's mansion, or hitch a ride on an antique steam train. Not only that, but you can see just about any world-class performance you'd like at many of the state's auditoriums and theaters. As more than one newcomer has discovered, there's a heck of a lot to do here.

Higher Education

UNIVERSITIES

One source of cultural activities is the University of Maine System (www.maine.edu), a group of seven distinct institutions located across the state. A common board of trustees and a chancellor oversee the schools, but each university has its own president, faculty, and administration.

The system's flagship school is located in Orono, twelve miles from Bangor, and is called simply the University of Maine, or "UMaine" (www.umaine.edu). It is a four-year residential university with five colleges—Business, Public Policy and Health; Education and Human Development; Engineering; Liberal Arts and Science; and Natural Sciences, Forestry, and Agriculture. It's particularly well known for its forestry and engineering departments, and by all accounts, UMaine is thriving. The class that hit the books in the fall of 1999 was 15 percent larger than the one that started in 1998 and 42 percent larger than the one that started in 1997.

Residents enjoy many benefits due to the university's presence. World-class performances at the Maine Center for the Arts, three on-campus museums, and Division I sports teams (including the 1999 NCAA champion men's hockey team) are just a few examples.

The second largest institution in the University of Maine System, the University of Southern Maine (USM), offers graduate degrees in law, business, computer science, manufacturing management, and many other fields. USM (www.usm.maine.edu) is a major force in southern Maine's business community, offering special courses, training programs, computer learning centers, technical assistance, and research services. The university is also a cultural power, sponsoring performances of all kinds and offering adult-ed classes and free lectures to the public.

The other University of Maine campuses also contribute much to their surrounding communities: drama, dance, and music performances; art exhibits and museums; sporting events; access to services such as libraries and athletic facilities; and, of course, the opportunity for lifelong learning. As proof of the public support for the University System, Maine voters approved a $20-million research and development bond referendum in 1998.

Another institution that is making more and more contributions to the culture of southern Maine is the University of New England, an independent, coeducational school whose charter dates back to 1831. The university (www.une.edu) has two distinct campuses—the main campus is located on a beautiful oceanside site in Biddeford while the Westbrook College Campus is in Portland.

The University of New England has graduate and undergraduate degree programs focused on the health and life sciences, human services, management, education, and the liberal arts. It also is home to Maine's only medical school, the University of New England College of Osteopathic Medicine, which emphasizes the education of primary-care physicians.

COLLEGES

Maine is also home to many fine colleges. Three—Bates, located in Lewiston, Bowdoin, in the heart of Brunswick, and Colby, overlooking Waterville—are listed among the top twenty-five liberal arts colleges in the nation. Others, such as the College of the Atlantic in Bar Harbor, Husson College in Bangor, and Maine College of Art in Portland, bring inquisitive learners to the state and offer residents a wealth of activities to enjoy. From free lectures on wellness to performances of Macbeth, from jazz ensembles to modern dance performances, these small colleges alone have enough cultural and educational activities to keep anyone happily stimulated most of the year. Some—such as Bowdoin College—even allow area seniors to audit courses at no charge.

There are also seven technical colleges (www.mtcs.tec.me.us) serving the entire state. Through the innovative Maine Quality Centers program, the schools recruit, screen, and train potential employees for companies that create new jobs in Maine—at no cost to either the employer or the trainee. The technical college system also helps prepare Maine's future workforce through initiatives such as the Maine Career Advantage, a partnership of

MAINE'S HIGHER EDUCATION INSTITUTIONS

UNIVERSITIES:
University of Maine at Augusta
University of Maine at Farmington
University of Maine at Fort Kent
University of Maine at Machias
University of Maine (Orono) (www.umaine.edu)
University of Maine at Presque Isle
University of New England
University of Southern Maine

COLLEGES:
Bates College, Lewiston (www.bates.edu)
Bowdoin College, Brunswick (www.bowdoin.edu)
Central Maine Technical College (www.cmtc.edu)
Colby College, Waterville (www.colby.edu)
College of the Atlantic, Bar Harbor (www.coa.edu)
Kennebec Valley Technical College, Fairfield
Maine Maritime Academy, Castine (www.mainemaritime.edu)
Northern Maine Technical College, Presque Isle
Southern Maine Technical College, Portland
St. Joseph's College
Thomas College, Waterville
Unity College
Washington County Technical College, Calais

COMMUNITY COLLEGES:
Andover College, Portland

Maine high schools and businesses. And frequently, these schools offer opportunities for community enrichment in activities such as continuing education and exhibits.

BANGOR THEOLOGICAL SEMINARY

Built in the 1800s, Bangor Theological Seminary (www.bts.edu) is an ecumenically based institution affiliated with the United Church of Christ that prepares men and women for the ministry. Headquartered in Bangor but with an additional campus in Portland, the school offers academic programs leading to degrees of Master of Divinity, Master of Theological Studies, and Doctor of Ministry.

In keeping with the school's larger vision to be a place where inquiry about the critical issues of society can evolve, the school offers workshops, symposia and public forums. Bangor Theological Seminary is the only accredited theological institution in northern New England.

VIRTUAL CLASSROOMS

Years ago, people living in isolated villages had little access to higher education. Beginning in the 1980s, the University of Maine System introduced a distance-learning network using television programming that connected Mainers from Kittery to Fort Kent with dozens of college courses and degrees. Today, people throughout the state pursue professional training or follow lifelong dreams through challenging distance-education courses and supportive university centers.

The growth of the Internet (and Maine's eighty-thousand miles of fiber-optic cable) has given long-distance learning another boost in the form of online courses and virtual classrooms. Soon Maine may even have its first online university, www.PortlandCollege.edu. The school calls itself "the University of Where You Are," and hopes to make a college education accessible to even more Mainers. The school is awaiting approval from the Maine legislature for degree-granting authority before issuing its first virtual diplomas.

ADULT EDUCATION

An incredible array of courses are available through local high schools and community centers. From stargazing to massage therapy, conversational

154

Italian to Public Speaking 101, Maine residents can brush up on subjects or become immersed in entirely new fields of study—and at a very reasonable cost. Look in the phone book under school districts for adult ed offerings in your area.

Maine Public Broadcasting

The Maine Public Broadcasting Corporation takes its mission to engage the minds and enrich the lives of Mainers seriously. Available to all Maine people every day, the corporation was created in 1992 with the merger of Maine's two public broadcasting systems (WCBB, founded by Colby, Bates, and Bowdoin colleges in 1961; and MPBN, founded by the University of Maine System).

The Maine Public Broadcasting Corporation broadcasts award-winning television (Maine PBS) and radio programming, creates special programs for Maine's schools and businesses, and has an excellent website (www.mpbc.org/index.html). A recent statewide vote—passed by nearly 65 percent of those who voted—earmarked funds for the corporation's transition from analog to digital in the twenty-first century.

Maine Public Television broadcasts about nineteen hours a day on Channel 10 in central Maine, Channel 26 in southern Maine, Channel 12 in northern Maine, and Channel 13 in eastern Maine. Its broadcast area covers the entire state, even venturing into New Hampshire and New Brunswick. All in all, Maine PBS covers an area of approximately five hundred thousand households.

In addition to carrying the popular PBS programs such as *Nova* and *Masterpiece Theatre,* Maine Public Television produces a substantial amount of original programming on local people and local issues. Among the local productions Mainers tune in to are: *Made in Maine, MaineWatch, True North, Capitol Connection, e-maine, RFD Maine, Quest: Investigating the World We Call Maine,* as well as the station's annual ten-day fund-raising auction, now in its twenty-sixth year, an April extravaganza featuring goods and services from around the state.

Maine Public Radio hit the airwaves in 1970. It broadcasts on six FM stations throughout the state: 89.7 Calais, 90.1 Portland, 90.9 Bangor, 91.3 Waterville, 106.1 Presque Isle, and 106.5 Fort Kent. More than one hundred and twenty thousand listeners each week enjoy comprehensive local news coverage, classical music, and programming from National Public Radio and Public Radio International. Many Mainers are devoted listeners, and MPR is a frequent winner of broadcasting awards.

Libraries

Maine's libraries are precious pearls scattered throughout the state. Many are housed in historic buildings that speak volumes about the state's history with their presence alone. All are linked through technology in a high-tech Internet necklace of information that makes researching and learning a snap. Maine's librarians just may be the most knowledgeable in the country,

The Raymond H. Fogler Library at the University of Maine (Orono) is the largest in the state, with nearly eight hundred thousand books and bound journals, more than 1.5 million government documents, and subscriptions to nearly seven thousand periodicals. *Photo by David McLean, Dept. of Marketing, courtesy of University of Maine.*

or perhaps it is their willingness to be helpful and pleasant that makes consulting them such a productive joy.

In addition to books, Maine's libraries big and small provide online assistance, access to periodicals, including magazines and newspapers, and they sponsor a host of public meetings and activities.

For a comprehensive list of the state's public, school, academic, state agency, and special libraries, check out Maine Libraries On-Line at: www .state.me.us/msl/melibson.htm. Many local libraries have their own web pages, so you can see what's going on in specific institutions around the state.

Cultural Activities

Below is a sampling of cultural offerings available throughout the state. While this list is by no means complete, it gives a good idea of the variety of opportunities available at all times of the year. Phone numbers are provided so you can check on particulars.

THEATER

Since the days of nineteenth-century summer theater, Mainers have enjoyed all kinds of theatrical performances, from Shakespeare under the stars to old time vaudeville to modern one-acts. There are professional companies, festivals with touring productions, and civic theaters where the local chief of police may have the starring role. Venues include historic old opera houses, converted churches and train stations, as well as more conventional auditoriums and theaters. Check out this website for more ideas: (www.summer theatre.com/Region/Northeast/maine.html). Here's a peek at what's available.

- *The Belfast Maskers Theatre,* Belfast. This group performs in a converted station house on the old Belfast/Moosehead railroad along the Belfast waterfront. Luminaries who have appeared with the Maskers over their twelve-year history include Liv Ullman and Ali Magraw. 207-338-9668; www.belfastmaskers.com.
- *Camden Civic Theatre,* Camden. This talented ensemble of local actors performs year round in the restored Camden Opera House, an elegant setting for entertainment of all types in the heart of downtown. Recent productions included *On Golden Pond* and *Fame.* 207-236-2281.

▲ ***Chamber Theatre of Maine,*** Damariscotta. Once called "the best-kept entertainment secret on the coast of Maine," the Chamber Theatre performs a variety of shows at the Round Top Center for the Arts. 207-354-8807.

▲ ***Deertrees Theatre and Cultural Center,*** Harrison. Nestled in the woods of western Maine, Deertrees is listed on both Maine's Register of Historic Landmarks and the National Register of Historic Places. The building was the dream of an opera coach from the New York Metropolitan Opera Company and was constructed in 1933 on the site of a former deer run. It was restored in 1984 through the efforts of a community group and hosts a variety of theatrical performances. 207-583-6747; www.lakesregionofmaine.gen.me.us/deertrees/

▲ ***Figures of Speech Theatre,*** Freeport. Figures of Speech is a seventeen-year-old, nationally known touring company whose actors are accompanied by live music and a cast of imaginative puppets. 207-865-6355.

▲ ***Lakewood Theatre,*** Skowhegan.The theater company at Lakewood has been performing for a century on tranquil Lake Wesserunsett, in a glen surrounded by a grove of towering birches. Productions include seven regular season plays, plus reprises, children's shows, and a theater camp for kids age six to sixteen years old. 207-474-7176.

▲ ***Mad Horse Theatre,*** Portland. One of the state's premier drama troupes, Mad Horse often performs in collaboration with local playwrights and USM students. 207-828-1270; www.madhorse.com.

A scene from a murder-mystery opera, *La Pizza Con Funghi,* presented by Opera Maine under the artistic directorship of David Katz, with the Chamber Orchestra of Maine. *Photo by Michael York, courtesy of Opera Maine.*

- **Maine State Music Theater,** Brunswick. Maine's only professional music theater has been playing to sell-out crowds for more than forty years. The group performs favorite musicals in the newly renovated Pickard Theatre on the campus of Bowdoin College. 207-725-8769; www.msmt.org.

- **Ogunquit Playhouse,** Ogunquit. "America's Foremost Summer Theatre" offers ten weeks of productions in a 750-seat restored, converted barn. Since opening in 1933, the cast of performers in the outstanding productions at the Playhouse has included Lee Remick, Basil Rathbone, Art Carney, and scores of others. 207-646-5511; www.oqunquitplayhouse.org.

- **Penobscot Theatre Company,** Bangor. In 1997, the Penobscot Theatre acquired the historic Bangor Opera House, a beautiful locale built in 1888. Performances are held there, as well as outside on the banks of the Penobscot River during the warmer months. 207-942-3333; http://maineguide.com.

- **The Theatre At Monmouth,** Monmouth. Designated by the state legislature in 1975 as "The Shakespearean Theatre of Maine," this company presents the work of the old bard in the century-old Cumston's Hall. It's an intimate setting (275 seats) in which plays are performed in rotating repertory. 207-933-9999; www.theatreatmonmouth.

ART

Over the last century, Maine has become synonymous with fine art, having inspired generations of internationally recognized artists such as Rockwell Kent, Winslow Homer, Marsden Hartley, Louise Nevelson, and the Wyeth family. It also is home to a handful of world-famous art colonies, like those at Ogunquit and Monhegan. Works by famous artists are in many collections across Maine, and there are also a dozen or so fine galleries along the length of the coast where you might find as yet unknown masterpieces. Here are a few of the outstanding museums that make up the state's newly formed Maine Art Trail, as well as a handful of more unusual offerings.

- **Bates College Museum of Art.** The prints, drawings, and paintings of Marsden Hartley, a Lewiston native, are featured in this collection, along with a variety of works by other well-known artists, including

159

Alex Katz, Alan Bray, and Ann Lofquist. 75 Russell Street, Bates College, Lewiston. 207-786-6158; abacus.bates.edu/acad/museum.

⚐ *Bowdoin College Museum of Art.* Here you'll find one of the earliest collegiate collections in America, with art from ancient Greece, Rome, and Asia, as well as European and American works representing a broad time period. Walker Art Building, Bowdoin College, Brunswick. 207-725-3275; www.bowdoin.edu/cwis/resources/museums.html.

⚐ *Colby College Museum of Art.* Twentieth-century American artists including John Marin, Fairfield Porter, and George Bellows are show-cased here, along with a large collection of works by Alex Katz. The museum also features early portraiture by John Singleton Copley, Gilbert Stuart, and Charles Wilson. 5600 Mayflower Hill, Colby College, Waterville. 207-872-3228; www.colby.edu/museum.

⚐ *Farnsworth Art Museum.* A focus on art created in or inspired by Maine has earned the Farnsworth recognition as one of the finest regional art museums in the country. Works by Fitz Hugh Lane, Rockwell Kent, and Louise Nevelson are part of the permanent col-lection, but the biggest attraction is the museum's new Wyeth Center, which boasts the world's largest collection of art by N.C., Andrew, and Jamie Wyeth. 356 Main Street, Rockland. 207-596-6457; www.farnsworthmuseum.org.

⚐ *Jones Museum of Glass and Ceramics.* A unique and very respected mu-seum in the world of glass, the Jones Museum features more than seven thousand works in the permanent collection, plus a research library and gallery shop. 35 Douglas Mountain Road, Sebago. 207-787-3370.

⚐ *Museum of African Tribal Art.* More than one thousand years of African history are represented in this world-class collection of tribal masks and artifacts. 122 Spring Street, Portland. Email: jaleshi1.

⚐ *Nowetah's American Indian Museum.* Genuine American Indian art from all parts of the U.S., Canada, and South America, plus a collec-tion of more than three hundred old Maine Indian sweetgrass/brown ash split baskets. New Portland. 207-628-4981.

⚐ *Ogunquit Museum of American Art.* More than thirteen hundred paint-ings, sculptures, drawings, and prints by Marsden Hartley, Edward Hopper, Walter Kuhn, and other twentieth-century American artists are shown here in a delightful setting with beautiful grounds. The

160

many painters of the famous Ogunquit art colony are, of course, well represented. 183 Shore Road, Ogunquit. 207-646-4909.

⚓ *Portland Museum of Art.* The state's best-known museum has gained world renown with the gift of the Joan Whitney Payson Collection of Impressionist and Post-Impressionist works by Renoir, Degas, Monet, Picasso, and other masters. The heart of the museum's is the State of Maine Collection, which features the work of such Maine artists as Winslow Homer, Edward Hopper, Rockwell Kent, John Marin, Maurice Prendergast, and Andrew Wyeth. Special exhibits and programs include a collection of fine and decorative arts dating from the nineteenth century to the present. The museum also hosts traveling exhibitions. 7 Congress Square, Portland. 207-775-6148; www.portlandmuseum.org.

⚓ *University of Maine Museum of Art.* Highlights include works by Winslow Homer, Francisco Goya, and Pablo Picasso, as well as works on paper by David Hockney, Roy Lichtenstein, and Elizabeth Murray. 5712 Carnegie Hall, UMaine, Orono. 207-581-3255; http://umna .umecah.maine.edu.

MUSIC

The music scene in Maine is as lively a mix as can be found anywhere: chamber and choral groups, chanty singers, blues artists, fiddle players, rock bands, several orchestras, and a bevy of music festivals. This incredible

The Bangor Symphony Orchestra, under the direction of Christopher Zimmerman, Music Director and Conductor. *Photo courtesy of Bangor Symphony Orchestra.*

diversity has prompted the Maine Arts Commission to award a $25,000 grant to the Maine Performing Arts Network to launch a statewide network of musicians similar to the successful Maine Art Trail.

The Maine Music Trail program aims to increase the awareness and appreciation of Maine's rich music heritage, as well as current music offerings. The "trail" will include educational, historical, and cultural components as well as a webpage and brochures.

"Maine is incredibly vibrant musically," says Kathy Hammond of the Portland Symphony Orchestra. "There's a lot to do here, and a great variety of types of music, including folk, ethnic, and classical. Maine offers ways for music lovers to observe, and ample opportunities for musicians to play."

ORCHESTRAS

Maine has a number of orchestras, based in Augusta, the midcoast, southern Maine, and at university campuses around the state. And there are two professional symphonies: the Bangor Symphony Orchestra and the Portland Symphony Orchestra.

The Bangor Symphony Orchestra's first performance was in November 1896, making the group the oldest continuously performing community orchestra in the United States. Today's performances are held at the Hutchins Concert Hall at the Maine Center for the Performing Arts in Orono, a venue with remarkable acoustics and not a bad seat in the house. The symphony is currently composed of ninety members, most of whom live within the state and have full or part-time jobs in addition to their musical careers. (One is a lobsterman.) The BSO's conductor is Christopher Zimmerman, chosen in 1994 from a field of three hundred applicants. Favorite performances by the orchestra include Beethoven's Ninth Symphony, accompanied by a two hundred-voice chorus. For more information call 207-942-5555 or visit the website, www.bangorsymphony.com.

Not quite as old but just as beloved, the seventy-six-year-old Portland Symphony Orchestra performs at Merrill Auditorium, home of the famous Kotzschmar Organ, one of the largest pipe organs in the world. The PSO is a $2.6-million dollar orchestra, offering fifty-six full concerts each year under the direction of conductor Toshiyuki Shimada. In addition, the group performs more than one hundred other programs, including Mozart & More, informal concerts celebrating the genius of Mozart. For lighter fare, the orchestra's pops concerts present offerings as diverse as swing dance music, Broadway hits, Hollywood favorites, and the familiar music of Rodgers and Hammerstein. For more information call 207-842-0800 or visit the PSO's website at www.portlandsymphony.com.

MORE MUSIC

♦ *Bay Chamber Concerts.* A series of classical music concerts have been held in the Rockport Opera House, winter and summer, in the midcoast community since 1961. Rockport. 207-236-2823; www.baychamber concerts.org.

♦ *Cormorant Chamber Players of Maine.* A small but lively combo based in Boothbay Harbor. 207-633-3936.

♦ *Center for the Arts at the The Chocolate Church.* An eclectic mix of music (including folk) and theater is offered at this Bath landmark year round. 207-442-8455.

♦ *Machias Bay Chamber Concerts.* Ensemble performances are held each summer in the historic Center Street Congregational Church. Machias. 207-255-3889.

♦ *Maine Music Society.* The Society presents the Androscoggin Chorale and Maine Chamber Ensemble in a series of choral and orchestral performances throughout the year. They also offer the Summer Chamber Music Series with educational outreach programs in the Lewiston/Auburn area. 207-782-1403; www.mainemusicsociety.org

♦ *Round Top Center for the Arts.* Damariscotta. 207-563-1507.

OPERA

♦ *The Gilbert and Sullivan Society of Hancock County.* Each year the society produces a Gilbert and Sullivan comic opera, six in winter and three in summer. The cast, crew, and orchestra are all volunteers. Ellsworth. 207-667-9500; http://ellsworthme/org/gsshc.

♦ *Portland Opera Repertory Theatre.* PORT performs in the newly refurbished Merrill Auditorium to sell-out crowds of opera fans. The past season's production was an elaborate performance of Puccini's *La Boheme.* Portland. 207-767-0773; www.portopera.org.

♦ *Opera Maine.* Unlikely though it may seem, Maine's professional opera company is based about as far from a city as it could be—in the tiny

Down East village of Steuben. But it's recognized for exceptional performances of opera, chamber music, recitals, and educational programs. Directed by noted professionals and featuring international, award-winning casts, Opera Maine is one of the fastest-growing arts organizations in the state. Steuben. 207-546-4495.

DANCE

Many Mainers enjoy dancing, both as performers and as spectators. Grange halls host foot-stomping contra dances, folk dances, and square dances, and studios for jazz, ballet, tap, swing, ballroom, and African dancing are found around the state. Here are just a few of the many performance offerings.

⚓ *Maine State Ballet.* Established in 1986, the Maine State Ballet has quickly become the leading professional dance company in the state. In cooperation with the Maine State School for the Performing Arts, the Maine State Ballet educates, entertains, and enriches the community through varied dance programs, including full-length ballets and one-act productions. The company is accompanied by the Maine State Ballet Orchestra. Portland. 207-842-0800; www.mainestateballet.org.

⚓ *Ram Island Dance Company.* One of the state's best-known modern troupes, Ram Island offers performances at venues around the state. Portland. 207-773-2562.

⚓ *Robinson Ballet.* Headquartered in Bangor's River City Dance Center, the Robinson company has been delighting audiences for more than twenty years, including popular annual Christmas performances of the *Nutcracker*. Bangor. 207-942-1990.

Schools and Workshops

Want to try your hand at a new art form? Build a dory or a highboy? Maine is home to many quality programs for everything from language study to ceramics. Here are a few ideas.

⚓ *Apprenticeshop of Rockland.* Here's where you'll find highly respected boat-building courses along the shores of Penobscot Bay. Rockland. 207-596-0884; www.apprenticeshop.com.

The Apprenticeshop in Rockland teaches the fine art of boatbuilding.
Photo courtesy of the Camden Herald.

⚓ *Center for Furniture Craftsmanship.* A new school, the Center has
quickly earned a stellar reputation based on the skill and teaching
ability of its instructors. Rockport. 207-594-5611; www.woodschool.org.

⚓ *Haystack Mountain School of Crafts.* A nationally known school offering two- and three-week workshops in visual arts and craft media.
Faculty work is on display periodically. Deer Isle. 207-348-2306;
www.haystack-mtn.org

⚓ *The Landing School of Boatbuilding and Design.* A full-time vocational
school, this southern Maine facility offers courses in yacht design
and boat building. Arundel. 207-985-7976; www.by-the-sea.com/
thelandingschool.

⚓ *Maine College of Art.* Right in the center of downtown, the Maine College of Art invigorates Portland's "Arts District" with young and enthusiastic artists and a well-regarded faculty. Portland. 207-775-3052;
www/meca.edu.

⚓ *Penobscot School.* The Penobscot School was founded in 1986 as a
nonprofit language school and center for international exchange, and
it has attracted people from around the world to the small city of
Rockland. Programs include summer English immersion for adults

165

from away, foreign language immersion weekends for Mainers and visitors, and weekly classes—from beginner to advanced—in many languages. Rockland. 207-594-1084; www.languagelearning.org.

⚑ *Rockport College/Maine Photographic Workshops.* Now in their twenty-sixth year, the Maine Photographic Workshops have an international reputation for courses in both photography and film. Top Hollywood players often pick up tricks of the trade right here in the little village of Rockport. 207-236-8581; www.theworkshops.com.

⚑ *Salzedo Harp School.* This unique school is a distinguished summer-long program for harpists from around the world. Camden. 207-236-2289.

⚑ *Skowhegan School of Painting and Sculpture.* A famous arts institution for serious students. Skowhegan. 207-474-9345; www.skowhegan art.org.

⚑ *WoodenBoat School.* The WoodenBoat School is an offshoot of the authoritative *WoodenBoat* magazine, and it's where serious aficionados go to build their dream vessel. Brooklin. 207-359-4651; www.wooden boat.com.

History Museums

Maine loves its rich history, as the number of history museums and historic buildings scattered across the state attest. These venerable institutions run the gamut from historic houses offering a well-preserved glimpse into the past to respected professional facilities with full-time staffs and research facilities. Some are open seasonally, so be sure to call before museum-hopping your way through the state. Here is a partial listing, for a complete list, check Maine Archives and Museums at www.mainmuseums.org or call them at 207-623-8428.

⚑ *Abbe Museum.* Located within Acadia National Park at Sieur de Monts Spring, this award-winning museum celebrates Maine's Native American heritage. Discover ten thousand years of culture, history, art, and archaeology through changing exhibits and workshops taught by Native American artists. Bar Harbor. 207-288-3519; www.abbemuseum.org.

Brick Store Museum. A history and art museum focusing on southern Maine with changing exhibitions and a semipermanent exhibition on Kennebunk and the Federal period. Kennebunk. 207-985-4802; www.cybertours.com/~brickstore/home.htm.

Burnham Tavern Museum. The tavern, built in 1770, features Revolutionary War information and artifacts. It was the staging point for the first naval battle of the war. Machias. 207-255-4432.

Center for Maine History. Part of the Maine Historical Society campus on Congress Street in Portland, the center features more than eight thousand items and hosts large-scale annual exhibitions. Portland. 207-774-1822; www.mainehistory.com.

College of the Atlantic Natural History Museum. The nature museum at this highly regarded ecology school features dioramas of animals and plants of Mount Desert Island, from foxes to finbacks. Bar Harbor. 207-288-5015; www.coa.edu.

Colonel Black Mansion. One of the few buildings in Maine that can rightly be called a mansion, this richly furnished Georgian-period home is known for its gracious gardens. Ellsworth. 207-667-8671; www.ellsworthme.org/cbmm/index.html.

Colonial Pemaquid. A unique collection from the Colonial era, Colonial Pemaquid is a sort of in-the-field archaeological museum situated as it is alongside on-going excavations. Pemaquid. 207-677-2423; www .state.me.us/doc/prkslands./prkslnds.htm.

Hudson Museum. On the campus of the University of Maine, this unusual museum—an anthropology collection featuring pre-Columbian artifacts—wraps around the Maine Center for the Arts. UMaine, Orono. 207-581-1901; www.ume.maine.edu/~hudsonm/.

The Kittery Historical and Naval Museum. The building of naval vessels in Kittery began during the Revolutionary War with the construction of John Paul Jones's sloop *Ranger* in 1777. The museum showcases a model of that vessel, plus artifacts galore depicting shipbuilding in the southernmost town in the state. Kittery. 207-439-3080.

Maine Folklife Center. An up-and-comer on Maine's museum scene, the Folk Life center showcases the folklore and oral history of the state. UMaine, Orono. 207-581-1891; www.umaine.edu/folklife/.

167

⚑ *Maine Forest and Logging Museum.* Just outside of Bangor, this is a living-history museum, a 265-acre property on which a late eighteenth-century logging operation is recreated. Leonard's Mills. 207-581-2871.

⚑ *Maine State Museum.* Located in the Capitol Complex in Augusta, the Maine State Museum features very detailed exhibits on all aspects of the state's history and culture from its earliest days. Many states have state museums—this one has a reputation as being among the best. Open daily, year-round. State Street, Augusta. 207-287-2301; http://janus.state.me.us/museum/.

⚑ *Moosehead Marine Museum.* The centerpiece of this upcountry, lake-side museum is the restored steamer *Katahdin,* which offers cruises on the state's largest lake every summer. Greenville. 207-695-2716.

⚑ *Museum of Vintage Fashion.* A highly regarded collection of antique clothing in The County, open seasonally. Island Falls. 207-862-3797.

⚑ *Norlands Living History Center.* Rural Maine life in the 1800s is re-lived on this 430-acre farm. Try the ninety-minute guided tour. Livermore. 207-897-4366; www.norlands.org.

⚑ *Patten Lumberman's Museum.* An outstanding collection of artifacts of the lumbering era in the Maine woods, this museum includes more than 3,000 artifacts displayed in nine buildings. Patten. 207-528-2650; www.lumbermensmuseum.org.

⚑ *Peary-MacMillan Arctic Museum.* This museum is filled with the photographs, diaries, and personal records of Admiral Robert Peary, the first man to reach the North Pole, and his assistant Donald MacMillan. Bowdoin College. Brunswick. 207-725-3062; www.bowdoin.edu/dept/arctic.

⚑ *Pownalborough Courthouse.* Not far from Wiscasset, this is the oldest pre-Revolutionary hall of justice in Maine. Dresden. 207-882-6817.

⚑ *Shaker Museum.* Maine is home to the only remaining colony of Shakers, and this small museum—right at their homestead—offers an excellent overview of life in a Shaker village. New Gloucester. 207-926-4597; www.shaker.lib.me.us/.

⚑ *Thompson's Ice House.* Back when ice was an industry, Thompson's was a player. Now you can see ice cut the old fashioned way at a site on the National Register of Historic Places. South Bristol. 207-729-1956.

Maritime Museums

Few places have as rich a seafaring legacy as does Maine, and the state displays its salty heritage proudly at a handful of institutions.

⚓ *Maine Maritime Academy.* While not exactly a museum, Maine Maritime Academy's training ship *State of Maine* is living history. Tour it and the school, too. Castine. 207-326-4311; www.mainemaritime.edu.

⚓ *Maine Maritime Museum.* With its collections and exhibitions, Maine Maritime Museum interprets the role of Maine ships and sailors in national and international maritime affairs since 1607. The museum's centerpiece is the Maritime History Building, where an extensive collection of artifacts, ship models, portraits, photographs, and memorabilia is displayed. The thirty-thousand-square-foot building is adjacent to the restored Percy & Small Shipyard, which may be the only

Maritime museums highlight the history of seafaring vessels such as these, tied up at a Portland wharf in 1882. *Photo courtesy of The Island Institute.*

169

wooden shipbuilding yard from the nineteenth-century still in existence in the U.S. Once majestic four-, five-, and six-masted schooners
were built here, and today, wooden boats are still crafted in the yard.
The museum's excursion boat *Summertime* makes several cruises along
the adjacent Kennebec River, adding a nice dimension to an entertain-
ing and educational visit. Open year round. Bath. 207-443-1316;
www.bathmaine.com.

▲ *Penobscot Marine Museum.* Much of the seafaring activity that built
this nation's early economy began in the Penobscot Bay region. This
museum, right on Route 1 in Searsport, features a pristine collection
of marine paintings, small craft, and artifacts that trace the history of
boat building in area. The collections and exhibits are housed in eight
historic structures, including the newly renovated Captain Jeremiah
Merithew House (1816), home to a fine collection of twenty-five
marine paintings by noted artists James and Thomas Buttersworth.
Both children and adults will enjoy the Fowler-True-Ross House, a
nineteenth-century sea captain's home reflecting family life and the
treasures brought back from many voyages. In the Nichols-Colcord-
Duncan Barn, the museum's collection of recreational small craft and
local fishing vessels are showcased. Searsport. 207-548-2529;
www.penobscotmarinemuseum.org.

▲ *Shore Village Museum.* The state's largest collection of lighthouse and
Coast Guard artifacts are at this unique museum on Limerock Street
in Rockland. Items include rare lighthouse lenses, working lights,
buoys, fog horns, bells, lifesaving, and lighthouse equipment. The
museum also has lighthouse and ship models, a permanent exhibit of
Civil War uniforms and weapons, and a Liewella Mills doll collection
complete with costumes, from circa 1399 to 1890. Rockland. 207-
594-0311; www.lighthouse.cc/shorevillage/index.html.

Transportation Museums

See an antique biplane zoom overhead, take a bumpy ride on a Model T, or
feel the wind in your hair as a steam engine train chugs through the countryside. Maine has an extensive collection of transportation museums, with
everything but lunar modules on display.

⁂ *Boothbay Railway Village.* A summer favorite in the Boothbay area, this museum is a miniature village and includes a fine collection of antique cars and a narrow-gauge railroad. Boothbay Harbor. 207-633-4727; www.railwayvillage.org.

⁂ *Cole Land Transportation Museum.* If it is an industrial vehicle that was once put to work in Maine, it can be found in this Bangor museum. A fine collection of antique trucks and accessories. Bangor. 207-990-3600; www.classicar.com/museums/coleland/cole.htm.

⁂ *Maine Narrow Gauge Railroad.* Narrow-gauge trains once crisscrossed Maine. The two-footers operated from rural areas, hauling slate, wood, and farm products to standard-gauge trains for shipment to markets around the world. The Trust for the Preservation of Maine Industrial History and Technology brought some of these vehicles back to Maine from the Edaville Railroad Museum in Massachusetts in 1993. Inside the museum are a 1913 locomotive, seven passenger cars, and much more. Portland. 207-828-0814; http://mngrr.railS.net/.

⁂ *Maine Watercraft Museum.* One of the best-kept secrets in the midcoast area, this museum houses watercraft built prior to 1960. There are more than one hundred antique and classic craft on display, including Old Town canoes. Open seasonally. Thomaston. 207-354-0444; www.midcoast.com/~oldboats.

⁂ *Owls Head Transportation Museum.* An institution on the midcoast, this museum boasts one of the finest collections of landmark aircraft and pre-1930 vehicles to be found anywhere. Pioneer engines, automobiles, carriages, bicycles, and motorcycles are maintained in operating condition and demonstrated during weekend special events and airshows, attracting visitors from all around the Northeast. (Hundreds bring their own pre-1970 vehicles to exhibit.) Highlights include World War I fighter planes, the Red Baron's Fokker Triplane, and a full-scale replica of the Wright Brothers' famous 1903 flyer. Road machines include a 1914 Rolls-Royce Ghost limousine and a restored Model T bus ready for riders. Open all year. Owls Head. 207-594-4418; www.ohtm.org.

⁂ *Seal Cove Auto Museum.* This often overlooked collection features more than one hundred antique autos, including Edsels. Seal Cove. 207-244-9242.

⚓ *Seashore Trolley Museum.* More than 200 transit vehicles, many operational, including MBTA trolleys, wooden cars from Europe, old New England horse drawn cars and much more are featured at this south coast institution. Kennebunkport. 207-967-2800; www.trolley museum.org.

⚓ *Stanley Museum.* This small museum features famous Stanley Steamer cars, invented by the twin brothers Stanley from right here in Kingfield. Also displayed are fascinating antique photographs by the Stanley's sister, Chansonetta Stanley Emmons, a pioneering shutterbug. Kingfield. 207-265-2729; www.stanleymuseum.org.

⚓ *Wells Auto Museum.* Some eighty restored autos, many of them built before 1915, including a large display of "Brass Era" antique cars are housed here. (After 1915, manufacturers turned from polished brass to painted headlamps, radiators and trim.) Wells. 207-646-9064; www.classicar.com/museums/wells/wells.htm.

Festivals and Fairs

Maine is the home of scores of wonderful celebrations. Some spotlight talented musicians, artists, and dancers, while others highlight the state's seafaring or agricultural heritage. Still others celebrate Maine's variety of cultures. Whatever the reason, if you're a fan of festivals or fairs, you're sure to find something to your liking. Here's a selection of offerings. For more information, see the Maine Tourism Association's calendar of events at www.mainetourism.com, or call them at 207-623-0363.

⚓ *Acadian Festival.* Way up in The County, this annual June gathering celebrates the local French-Acadian culture through music. St. John Valley. 207-728-7000; www.madawaska.net.

⚓ *Annual Maine Indian Basket Makers Sale and Demonstration.* This December event takes place at the Hudson Museum on the University of Maine campus. It features Maliseet, Micmac, Passamaquoddy, and Penobscot craftspeople who sell their hand-made, one-of-a-kind, ash splint and sweet grass basketry. Work baskets, such as creels, pack and potato baskets, and curly bowls may be found along with quill jewelry, wood carvings, and birch bark work. Traditional foods served up by the Indian Island Cafe, storytelling and flute music, and demonstrations of brown ash pounding are also presented. Orono. 207-581-1901.

♠ *Common Ground Fair.* The Common Ground Fair is held each fall in late September to celebrate rural living. Sponsored by the Maine Organic Farmers and Gardener's Association, the fair is three days of music, farm displays, children's activities, and wonderfully tasty organic food. The sheep dog demonstrations are always popular. Unity. 207-623-5155; www.mofga.org.

♠ *La Kermesse Festival.* A four-day Franco-American festival held in late June, La Kermesse features a parade, block party, and loads of entertainment. Biddeford. 207-286-3247.

♠ *Maine Festival.* Produced by Maine Arts, Inc., this is a four-day, multifaceted art and cultural festival, founded twenty years ago by the late Maine storyteller Marshall Dodge. Held annually in early August, there are workshops, demonstrations, music, food, and entertainment galore. The festival grounds are handicapped accessible. Thomas Point Beach, Brunswick. 207-772-9012; www.mainearts.org/festhome.html.

♠ *Maine Lobster Festival.* A three-day extravaganza in early August, this well-loved festival features Maine's most famous crustacean. Highlights include a lively parade, big-name music acts (Willie Nelson, for example, in 2000), exhibits, and—you guessed it—pot after pot of steaming lobsters. Rockland. 207-596-0376; www.mainelobster festival.com.

♠ *Maine Potato Blossom Festival.* Hooray for Maine's spuds! This July event includes the crowning of the Potato Blossom Queen, a pageant, mashed potato wrestling, fireworks, and the thrilling 'Roostook River Raft Race. Fort Fairfield. 207-472-3802.

♠ *The Moxie Festival.* A wacky and fun festival featuring crafts, a parade, entertainment, and carnival rides, this July staple honors Maine's indigenous soft drink with the distinctive taste. Lisbon. 207-763-2249.

♠ *Schooner Days and North Atlantic Blues Festival.* Rockland gets rocking for a few days in July when nationally known blues artists show up and play. Crafts, fireworks, and a parade of sail round out the festivities. Rockland. 207-596-0376; www.midcoast.com/~bluesman/.

- *Thomas Point Beach Bluegrass Festival.* This shindig has enjoyed great popularity in recent years. It's held in early September and draws bluegrass fans around the state (and many from away, too). Thomas Point Beach, Brunswick. 207-725-6009.
- *Topsham Fair.* One of Maine's largest agricultural fairs, this great festival is held annually in August. Thousands show up for farm-related displays, harness racing, crafts, and home cooking. Topsham. 207-725-2735.
- *Yarmouth Clam Festival.* Bivalves get their day during mid-July, celebrated with a midway, parades, races, good eatin', and more. Yarmouth. 207-846-3984.
- *Union Fair and Blueberry Festival.* An old-fashioned agricultural fair with harness racing, pig scrambles, and a farm museum, plus a tasty festival celebrating Maine's tangy wild blueberry takes over the Union Fairgrounds every August. Union. 207-594-5563.

Conferences

Maine is the site of several exciting annual conferences. The state's universities and colleges sponsor conferences on every imaginable topic, such as the annual Women in Leadership Conference—featuring Maine's most dynamic leaders from business, politics, and education—held at Thomas College in Waterville.

Maine is also the kind of place where a group of people can organize a series of seminars and start something really exciting. For example, in 1989 a small group of people interested in world affairs—many of them because they were once deeply involved in such things—decided to organize a conference in the midcoast area. The event drew residents as well as government officials from around the globe who came together to hear lectures and participate in discussions. So successful was the Camden Conference (www.camdenconference.org) that it has continued every February for more than ten years, and has inspired a second series, held in October, featuring issues in technology (www.camcon.org).

9 Family Life

"I like this state's politics, which put families first."
—Lynda Chilton*

Best Place to Raise Kids

The recent news that Maine was voted the best state in the country to raise children by a Washington D.C.–based children's advocacy group did not come as a surprise to anyone living in the state. Even new residents are impressed with the kid-friendly policies, safe streets and cities, clean air, and old-fashioned sense of community. "In Maine, my nine- and six-year-old girls can be comfortable being kids," says Lynda Chilton, who moved to the state in 1998. "Having fun can mean chasing frogs all afternoon, or going to the corner shop with friends for ice cream. They can walk home from school or go to the library without parental supervision," she explains. "In Virginia, children were becoming mini grown-ups, with stresses and peer pressures that I didn't face when I was little."

Shortly after his election in 1994, Governor Angus S. King, Jr. established the Children's Cabinet. Made up of the commissioners of the five state agencies most closely involved with children and families, plus the governor and first lady Mary Herman, the group has worked since 1994 to organize the best services for Maine children, families, and communities. One 1997 initiative of the Cabinet, Communities for Children, has had a measurable impact. More than two hundred municipalities around the state participated by developing local councils that tapped into state resources to create prevention programs for problems such as substance abuse, youth violence, and teen pregnancy. The program also helped communities in the state connect and share information, through a website, publications, local training events, and statewide gatherings.

---

*Lynda Chilton, conversation with author.

THE TOP TEN PLACES TO RAISE A CHILD

1. Maine	6. North Dakota
2. Massachusetts	7. Maryland
3. Connecticut	8. Kansas
4. Vermont	9. Wisconsin
5. New Hampshire	10. Iowa

Source: 1999 annual report of the Children's Rights Council, Washington, D.C. The organization considered a variety of factors, including child immunization rates, the percentage of juvenile arrests, the number of mothers receiving prenatal care in the first trimester, divorce rates, and instances of child abuse and neglect. Maine has never placed lower than twelfth in the study, and in 1998 the state's ranking was eighth. Maine garnered the top spot in 1999, say officials, in part because of a series of initiatives for children established by Governor King's administration.

The success of Communities for Children and the Children's Cabinet has garnered Maine national recognition, from Vice President Al Gore's Partnership for Reinventing Government, the National Governor's Conference, and, of course, the 1999 designation by the Children's Rights Council. However, the best proof that these programs are working is in critical statistics like the following.

Maine can claim:

- The lowest infant mortality rate in the nation.
- The highest immunization rate in the nation.
- The third-lowest teen birth rate in the nation.
- The greatest decline (30 percent) in teen birth rates in the nation from 1991 to 1996.
- The highest rate (90 percent) of women receiving prenatal care in the nation.
- The lowest number of families currently on public assistance since 1970.

These important baselines help ensure that every Maine child has a healthy start.

More serious concerns aside, there is something magical about Maine and children. Think back to your childhood. Can you remember what mattered most to you? I have always loved roaming beaches, tromping through the woods, and spying on wildlife while canoeing on a quiet lake—fragments of time spent with family members in special, unhurried places. Maine is made for family recreation, for fun times that don't need to wait for a vacation.

Another special quality of life in Maine is the small-town atmosphere. Children are enriched by the community connections—the very real knowledge that grown-ups other than your parents know you, care about you, and will tell on you if you don't look when crossing the street. Security. Safety.

And snow. What child doesn't find the phenomenon of snowflakes swirling down to earth a marvelous, miraculous event? (Not to mention the chance to miss school.)

"Jason and I moved to Maine because of family ties, but also because we wanted to raise our kids in a place that was safe, normal, beautiful, and full of good folks," says Kristy Scher of Rockland. Maine is that place.

Kids and Safety

According to Maine law, all passengers in a moving car must be buckled up. As far as adults are concerned, the seatbelt law is a secondary law, which means a vehicle cannot be stopped just because a police office suspects the driver isn't wearing a seatbelt. Where children are involved, however, the law is tougher. All kids nineteen years old and under must be strapped into their safety belts, and since this law is mandatory, drivers can be pulled over for it. Maine law also states that children four years of age and younger must be in an approved child safety seat. Kids sixteen and under must also wear bicycle helmets when riding their bikes.

Health Care

State-of-the-art birthing centers are found in Maine's hospitals, with certified nurse midwives and doula services becoming increasingly common.

For serious pediatric concerns, The Barbara Bush Children's Hospital at Maine Medical Center offers a comprehensive array of services for children, including the inpatient unit and other services throughout the hospital and

The Barbara Bush Children's Hospital at Maine Medical Center offers all aspects of pediatric medicine for infants, young children, and teens. *Photo courtesy of Maine Medical Center.*

beyond. Other facilities around the state have pediatric wings, such as Eastern Maine Medical Center in Bangor, which boasts a brand-new twenty-four bed children's wing.

Adoption

Maine finalized more than 210 adoptions of children in state custody in 1999, a record number. But for the seven hundred Maine children still waiting to be adopted, that number isn't quite high enough.

A new Internet site designed to reach out to prospective adoptive parents may shorten the wait. The "Maine's Waiting Children" site (www .adopt.org/me) profiles Maine children awaiting adoptions and has a database search of eligible children, as well as a link to the National Adoption Center. All Maine children looking for adoptive parents will eventually be listed on the site.

Schools

Education is among any parent's top concerns when relocating to a new community. "We were really concerned about schools for Alex," says Jan Njaa of Belfast. "After talking with a school administrator and some parents we felt that Belfast would be a great place for her. We've been told there is a lack of activities for older kids, but we'll tackle that as it comes."

Maine has a progressive education system that is ranked among the top ten in the country. In fact, the K–12 system may very well be the best in the country. In December 1999, the National Educational Goals Panel recognized Maine as the state with the highest performance in the nation in improving public education. Among the strengths of Maine's schools are small class size (the average is fourteen students per teacher), high student engagement, and high parental involvement. Communities tend to be concerned about—and involved in—what goes on within the school's doors.

"Just after we moved here from Chicago, our daughter's elementary school was threatened with consolidation," says Jan Njaa. "The community voiced their concern and we were impressed with how much the parents and neighbors valued having the schools in the neighborhood. The building will be renovated instead. There's a real sense of community in Maine, and we feel like the quality of the education Alex will get will be high."

QUALITY SCHOOLS

Just where does Maine figure in terms of educational quality? Here are some facts from the Department of Education:

- Maine's fourth and eighth graders scored among the highest in the nation in math, reading, and science assessment tests.
- Maine's education system is ranked second in the United States in the "school climate" category according to *Education Week* in 1999.
- All of Maine's schools and libraries, nearly twelve hundred sites, are linked via Frame Relay Service, allowing Internet access.
- Maine exceeds the national average in education investment— the state is twelfth in the nation in education spending.
- Maine is ranked thirteenth in the nation for high school graduation rate.
- Maine was one of only eight states to receive a five-year, $12-million grant to launch a model education reform agenda.
- Maine ranks second, along with Utah, in the percent of education dollars that are spent directly to support instruction, a remarkable achievement given Maine's high cost for transportation and facilities due to its rural geography.

A 1997 study by *Forbes* magazine revealed that, in a nationwide comparison, Maine gets the biggest bang for its education buck. Per-pupil spending is near the national average even though Maine students have the highest composite scores on the National Assessment of Educational Progress (NAEP). As the Maine Department of Education itself notes, "Average investment and top performance—not a bad scorecard!"

Here are more facts provided by the Maine Department of Education (http://janus.state.me.us/education/homepage.htm):

- Only students in Singapore outperformed Maine eighth graders in science in comparisons with the 41 countries participating in the Third International Mathematics and Science Study (1998).
- Maine eighth graders came in eighth in mathematics in comparisons with the 41 countries participating in the Third International Mathematics and Science Study (1998).

Students from Rockport Elementary School learn about rare breeds of farm animals at Kelmscott Farm in Lincolnville. *Photo courtesy of Kelmscott Farm.*

- Maine eighth graders placed first in the nation in reading, and Maine fourth graders placed fourth in the nation in reading on the 1998 National Assessment of Educational Progress.
- Maine eighth graders placed first in the nation in science on the 1996 National Assessment of Educational Progress.
- Maine fourth graders placed first in the nation, along with Minnesota and Connecticut, in mathematics on the 1996 National Assessment of Educational Progress (NAEP).
- Eighth graders also placed first in the nation in math, along with North Dakota, Minnesota, Wisconsin, Montana, and Iowa on the 1996 test.

School Organization

Schools in Maine are under local control. Some towns and cities supervise their own schools individually, others combine and pool educational resources in school administrative districts (S.A.D.s) or community school districts (C.S.D.s). Most Maine schools are supervised by a school board or committee, which administers education through a superintendent of schools.

State Funded Schools

Three schools in Maine are directly funded by the state: the Governor Baxter School for the Deaf in Falmouth, the Maine School of Science and Mathematics in Limestone (Maine's only charter school), and the Arthur E. Gould School in South Portland.

Private Schools

There are 108 approved private schools in Maine, everything from Montessori schools to Waldorf to parochial schools. A few of these—like Lincoln Academy in the Damariscotta-Newcastle area—serve as public schools for local towns, which pay tuition for students. Size of student body varies: the Hilltop School in Bangor has only eighteen students, while Fryeburg Academy provides education for 530. For a complete list of approved schools, check this website: http://janus.state.me.us/education/eddir/homepage.htm.

Arts in the Schools

L/A Arts, an outfit that brings world-class talent to the twin cities of Lewiston and Auburn, sponsors an innovative program that puts performers and artists into the schools on a regular basis. So popular is the program that it has been copied in communities around Maine and served as a model for similar programs in other states.

Challenges Still to Be Met

There are family issues in Maine that need work, problems that the state and local communities are working hard to solve. "We've found so many plusses to living here," say Gordon and Carol Doherty-Cox of Port Clyde. "On the negative side, we were astonished at the amount of domestic abuse." Another newcomer, Gary Swanson, makes this observation: "Maine seems to have its share of dysfunctional individuals and families."

Children in Maine, like everywhere, are affected by poor parenting practices. In 1996, the Department of Human Services confirmed 4,656 substantiated cases of abuse and neglect. From 1992 to 1996, the number of children living in poverty was 15.8 percent, below the national average, but

MAINE SCHOOLS
SURF THE WEB

- Maine was the first state in the nation to successfully connect all of its public schools and public access libraries to the Internet.
- All schools and libraries that are connected to the Maine School Library Network receive unlimited use of the Internet at no cost.
- An advanced interactive television system is currently being piloted and is arguably the most advanced interactive video, voice, and data technology available. The proceeds from a statewide bond will allow this technology to be placed in every high school in Maine.

still cause for concern. Maine isn't perfect—no place is—and there are challenges to be met within the state's homes and schools.

For instance, although Maine students score at or near the top of the nation in mathematics, reading, and science, the Department of Education feels that one out of four students here has not acquired a level of literacy that is acceptable by most standards. Maine children may outperform the other states, but they are not performing up to their full potential as outlined in Maine's Learning Results standards.

According to the Maine Youth Risk Behavior Survey, 22 percent of Maine students are frequent cigarette users, higher than the national average of 17 percent. Of middle school students—grades seven and eight—21 percent smoked cigarettes on one or more occasions in the past thirty days. By high school the number rose to 39 percent. And in 1997, 41 percent of Maine children reported that someone had offered, sold, or given them an illegal drug on school property during the past year. So everything is not rosy Down East, but these are problems students face everywhere.

And finally, the Maine Department of Education is concerned that Maine students rank poorly when it comes to educational aspirations. Although Maine ranks thirteenth in terms of high school graduation, not enough young Mainers go on to post-secondary study. These issues are of critical importance to the state's families and future.

Kid-Friendly Activities

"My girls can do all of the activities they did in Virginia and more," says Lynda Chilton. The Chilton family relocated to the midcoast in April 1998 after lots of research and years of looking for the best place to raise their two daughters. "I wanted to make sure my family would not sacrifice anything from changing locations," explains Lynda. "I researched housing costs, available activities such as horseback riding and ballet, public and private schools, and business technology such as Internet access, multiple phone lines, and delivery services."

With information in hand, Lynda and her husband, Thad, realized they had no major concerns about relocating. "From visits here, we knew we loved the beauty and people of Maine," says Lynda. "We love the outdoors, and we enjoy real winters. The hard part became leaving my parents in

Children in Maine have the natural world in their backyards. Shells and crabs are among the interesting items to find at Warren Island State Park in Islesboro. *Photo by Victoria Doudera.*

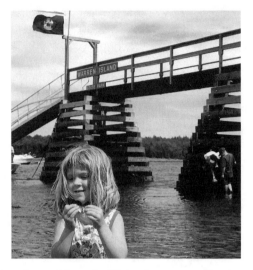

Virginia who lived only a few minutes away." Fortunately, Lynda's parents visit often and have even considered moving to Maine themselves. "People should think about what they really like to do and see if they can keep doing those things in Maine," suggests Lynda. "Most of Maine is small-town living, and that has a character all its own."

Dance classes, music lessons, art workshops, Kindermusik—Maine has it all, in a setting that is conducive to quality family time. In addition to the offerings listed in Chapter 7, here are a few more activities specifically for the young and young-at-heart.

THEATER

Theater for children ranges from the many puppetry groups to several troupes in which kids are cast in starring roles. Best known of these is the Children's Theatre of Maine, headquartered in Portland, which features year-round productions, plus a comedy troupe and improvisational classes. For more information call 207-878-2774.

MUSEUMS

Maine is home to several museums that offer children insight into the state's rich history, art, and culture. Some are listed in Chapter 8, but here are three specifically geared to the younger set.

▲ *The Children's Museum of Maine.* Three floors of interactive exhibits aimed at kids one through fourteen right in downtown Portland. The

184

lobster boat, mini space shuttle, and camera obscura are big hits. Portland. 207-828-1234; www.childrensmuseumofme.org.

▲ *Children's Discovery Museum.* This relatively new museum presents hands-on opportunities for children through grade five. Augusta. 207-622-2209.

▲ *Western Maine Children's Museum.* A family learning center providing exhibits which encourage child/adult interaction. Carrabassett Valley. 207-235-2211.

MUSIC

Gifted musicians abound in Maine, ready to instruct your child in his or her instrument of choice. In addition to lessons, though, there are remarkable concert series designed just for children. Here are a few options:

▲ *Kinderkonzerts.* These concerts by members of the Portland Symphony Orchestra bring live chamber music to preschool kids in Maine and New Hampshire. The children are introduced to the different families of orchestral instruments and the elements of music through audience participation, exciting demonstrations, and narration. Portland. 207-773-6128; www.portlandsymphony.com.

▲ *Portland Youth Concerts.* Held at Merrill Auditorium, these Portland Symphony Orchestra concerts introduce children ages seven through thirteen to the full symphony orchestra. 207-773-6128.

▲ *Bangor Youth Concerts.* The magic of live orchestral music—courtesy of the Bangor Symphony—is brought to more than four thousand school children from across the state. A highlight of each concert is a solo performance by the winner of the Bangor Symphony Orchestra's Maine High School Concerto Competition. Bangor. 207-989-2104; www.bangorsymphony.com.

▲ *The Bangor Symphony Youth Orchestra and Ensemble.* The BSO Youth Orchestra provides an opportunity for student musicians to play orchestral music of a quality unmatched by school programs and private instruction. The orchestra inspires the musicians' confidence, challenges their music abilities, and brings together peers who enjoy playing orchestral compositions. Bangor. 207-989-2104.

↟ *New England Music Camp.* A family-run music camp begun in 1937, New England Music Camp offers quality and intensive musical education with popular sports and recreational activities. A sort of summer camp with horns. Sidney. 207-465-3025.

SCOUTING AND 4-H

As a veteran den leader for Cub Scout Pack 200, one of Maine's largest and possibly most enthusiastic, I'd be remiss if I didn't mention scouting opportunities. Scouting for boys and girls is popular in the Pine Tree State, probably because of the many prime areas for top-notch outdoor activities. Hiking, tenting, canoeing, and swimming are all within a stone's throw for most scouts, and beautiful camping areas—some owned by the scouting councils—abound. The Pine Tree Council BSA oversees boy scouting in Maine. To contact the council, try their website at www.pinetreebsa.org or call 207-797-5252. For Girl Scout information, contact the Kennebec Valley Girl Scout Council at 800-660-1072.

Maine is also home to an active 4-H community, in which youngsters do such projects as raise livestock, make clothing, or grow vegetables. They then exhibit their efforts at fairs around the state. In Maine, 4-H is the youth development program of the University of Maine cooperative extension. For more information, call 207-581-3877 or see their website at www.umext.maine.edu/topics/4handyouth.htm.

SUMMER CAMPS

Thousands of children from across the country come to camp in Maine every summer. They roast marshmallows, learn the breaststroke, and laugh and sing in their platform tents until they absolutely cannot keep their eyes open. They make friendships that may last for years, and learn skills that stand them in good stead into adulthood.

Many of the nation's first summer camps were founded in Maine, and some are still run by second- and third-generation camp directors. Dr. Luther H. Gulick, one of the founders of the Camp Fire Girls, started several of Maine's first camps, and championed the idea that summer camps should provide both educational and recreational activities. For more information on children's summer camps, see the website of the Maine Youth Camping

Association at http://maine.maine.edu/~myca/ or call them at 207-581-1350 and request their free directory.

FORTS

What kid doesn't love a fort? Fortunately, Maine's got plenty. Here are a few to explore, but for more ideas, see the Maine Department of Conservation's listing at www.state.me.us/doc/parks.htm.

- ⚓ *Fort Edgecomb.* This octagonal blockhouse has beautiful picnicking grounds overlooking the Sheepscot River. Edgecomb. 207-882-7777.
- ⚓ *Fort Halifax.* This fort's blockhouse was built in 1754 and is the oldest in the United States. Winslow.
- ⚓ *Fort Kent.* This blockhouse was erected in 1840 as part of military preparations for what looked like an impending war against Canada. Fort Kent. 207-941-4014.

The cannon at Fort Knox State Historic Site in Prospect, the first granite fort built in Maine. *Photo courtesy of Bureau of Parks and Lands, Maine Department of Conservation.*

▲*Fort Knox Historical Site.* Perhaps the midcoast's best-known fort, Fort Knox was built in 1844 to protect citizens from the British, and it has underground passages that never fail to intrigue children. Prospect. 207-469-7719.

▲*Old Fort Western Museum.* A restored sixteen-room garrison house from 1755, Old Fort Western is listed as a National Historic Landmark and hosts many educational programs. Augusta. 207-626-2385.

▲*Fort William Henry.* Fort William Henry is a replica of a colonial fort with fantastic views across Pemaquid Harbor. Bristol. 207-677-2423.

▲*Fort Williams.* A very popular park in Greater Portland, Fort Williams has extensive grounds as well as some ruins that are fun to explore.

ANIMALS

▲*Kelmscott Farm.* A working farm dedicated to the conservation of endangered livestock breeds including Cotswold Sheep, Kerry Cows, Gloucestershire Old Spots Pigs, and much more. Open daily except Mondays, year round. Lincolnville. 207- 763-4088; www. kelmscott.org.

PROFILE

The Price family—Bob, Laurie, and their two daughters—moved to Maine in 1996 from Washington, D.C. "We'd wanted to relocate here for a long time," explains Bob, who is originally from Houston, Texas. "My wife is from Connecticut, but she has family in Eagle Lake. I'm active-duty military, and we were very pleased to be stationed in Caribou. From the first, we liked it up here. It's a laid-back, easy going lifestyle, and this is a great community that really welcomes people. There's no 'keeping up with the Joneses,' and the school system is very strong." Bob is actively trying to make Maine's educational system even better through his efforts with the State PTA Board. "Maine is the number-one place to raise kids," Bob Price says, "and if we focus on the future we can make Maine's schools unbeatable. We've got a clean environment, low crime, caring people, and real respect for each other in Maine. It's a great place to live."

The nostalgic clip-clop of hooves is often the only sound on a hayride.
Photo by Ken Bailey.

⚑ *Acadia Zoo.* A small zoo with one hundred and fifty animals plus a rainforest exhibit and petting area. Bar Harbor. 207-667-3244.

⚑ *The Maine Wildlife Park.* This park, managed by The Department of Inland Fisheries and Wildlife, is home to injured or orphaned animals such as bear, deer, lynx, and even a mountain lion. The park is located in Gray. Call 207-657-4977 for more information, or see their website at http://janus.state.me.us/ifw/education/wildlifepark.htm.

MAINE FOODS AND FARMS

One of the benefits of life in a rural state is the opportunity to visit working farms and orchards. Below are just a few places around the state where you can pick just about anything from blueberries to bush beans. More than one hundred pick-your-own farms open themselves to visitors, so for a complete list, check out the Maine Department of Agriculture's website at www.mainefoodandfarms.com or call 207-287-9072.

⚑ *Alheri Gardens.* Create bouquets from this Greater Portland farm's lovely gardens. Daffodils, tulips, peonies, and summer annuals are all available. Gray. 207-657-4358.

⚑ *Simons Hancock Farm.* Pick-your-own peas, beans, and pumpkins. Come fall, the farm offers hay rides to the pumpkin field, a big pumpkin smash, pumpkin weight guessing, and other games and amusements. Hancock. 207-667-1359.

↟*Dot Rupert's Strawberry Farm.* Tasty home of strawberries, raspberries, and highbush blueberries in the foothills of the western mountains. Hebron. 207-966-2721.

↟*Boutilier's Vegetables.* Pick-your-own vegetables way up in The County, including peas, beans, corn, tomatoes, carrots, beets, beet greens, and cucumbers. Island Falls. 207-757-8312.

APPLE ORCHARDS

Of the forty orchards listed with the Maine Department of Agriculture, thirty-two are classified as pick-your-own. Some even offer kids the chance to visit farm animals, see a cider press, or take a hayride. Here is a sampling:

↟*The Apple Farm.* Pumpkins, squash, cider, and apples ripe for the picking are the attraction here. Fairfield. 207-453-7656.

↟*Apple Ridge Farms.* One of Maine's largest orchards, this farm offers hayrides and farm animals. Auburn. 207-225-3455.

↟*County Fair Farm.* This Lincoln County farm has a full farm stand, a baby animal barn, and weekend hayrides. Jefferson. 207-549-3536.

↟*Lemieux's Orchards.* Cider is made right here at the orchard, and you'll find loads of apple varieties. North Vassalboro. 207-923-3518.

↟*Merrill Apple Farms.* Look for the cider press and other produce in addition to all the apples. Ellsworth. 207-667-5121.

↟*Spiller Farm.* Lots of varieties of apples await at this southern Maine farm, plus hayrides and garden veggies. Wells. 207-985-2575.

MAINE MAPLE SUNDAY

Every March the state celebrates one of spring's sweetest rites—the making of maple syrup. Sugar makers open the doors of their sugarhouses to demonstrate just how maple sap is turned into everyone's favorite pancake-topper. Many offer a variety of other treats and activities, including syrup on pancakes or ice cream, sugarbush tours, sleigh or wagon rides, and lots more. Maine Maple Sunday is always the fourth Sunday in March. For a list of participating sugarhouses, contact the Department of Agriculture at 207-287-9072 or visit the agency's website at www.mainefoodand farms.com.

10 Joining the Community

*"This is what I can't decide: whether I don't have any spare
time at all, or whether most of my time is spare time."*
—Louise Dickinson Rich*

How can you nourish your soul in Maine? Besides spending time enjoying nature, new residents find there are all kinds of community organizations that need and welcome participation. "There's plenty of opportunity for 'volunteer' employment," says Allie Lou Richardson of Islesboro. "I had worried that I was leaving all my friends, my church, and my community activities behind, but there's plenty to do, and welcoming, friendly people to do it with."

Many new residents find they enjoy giving back to their adopted communities through donating their time at service organizations, churches, and nonprofit groups. Still others train to become volunteer firefighters, docents at local museums, or directors on the board of the community YMCA. There are opportunities to mentor youth, maintain hiking trails, and care for wildlife. Once you've settled in a bit, town committees are another option for interested residents who want to see the inner workings of town politics.

Perhaps you enjoy ornamental or vegetable gardening. Each year, it seems, more and more Mainers spend their spare time enriching the soil and cultivating beautiful blooms. "I was told people don't garden much in Maine," says Jan Njaa of Belfast. "But now that I live here, I see that's clearly not the case." In spite of (or perhaps because of) a short growing season, Mainers love their gardens and enjoy ready access to a variety of services that support green thumbs. In addition, an ever-increasing number of farmers' markets have sprouted in all corners of the state, providing high-quality, delicious produce as well as inspiration.

----

*Louise Dickinson Rich, *We Took to the Woods*, J.B. Lippincott Co., 1942.

Church Life

"I'm surprised we've become so involved in church since moving to Maine," says Lynda Chilton. "We attended services in Virginia, but never were really a part of it. Here, it seems the churches are more integrated into the community. I think that's why there is such a good overall spirit here, and why kids seem to grow up more wholesome. Church is really a support to the family, and I like that."

Maine is a place of many faiths, too numerous to list completely. There are Presbyterian, Methodist, Congregational, Episcopalian, and Catholic churches along with Quaker Meeting Houses and Jewish synagogues. Many communities have Baptist and Unitarian-Universalist churches. And Eastern religions, while in the minority, are slowly growing. Most Maine congregations—regardless of faith—are small by city standards.

The Maine Council of Churches has a new 150-page directory that includes many of Maine's religious institutions, including synagogues, sorted

For more information on religious denominations in Maine, try these organizations:

American Baptist Churches of Maine, 207-622-6291
Assemblies of God, 207-878-2777
Church of the Nazarene, 207-623-4255
Congregational Christian Churches, 207-797-2487
Episcopal Diocese of Maine, 207-772-1953
Evangelical Lutheran Church, 508-791-1530
Jewish Federation of Maine, 207-773-7254
Maine Conference of the United Church of Christ,
    207-846-5118
Presbyterian Church U.S.A., 603-629-9900
Religious Society of Friends, 207-359-8090
Roman Catholic Diocese, 207-773-6471
United Methodist Church, 207-773-4375
Unitarian-Universalist Church, 207-797-3246

Saints Peter and Paul Church in Lewiston boasts twin spires and a majestic rose window reminiscent of Notre Dame. Construction of the magnificent building took thirty-two years—from 1906 until 1938—with mill workers scraping money together even during the Depression. *Photo by William Karz, courtesy of Androscoggin County Chamber of Commerce.*

by county and town. Call them for more information at 207-772-1918. Here are profiles of some of Maine's larger religious groups.

Maine's Roman Catholic population grew rapidly with the influx of Irish immigrants in the early 1800s, and then, following the Civil War, with the large numbers of French Canadians who came to work in the mills. Today about one-quarter of Maine's people are Roman Catholic, worshipping in 191 churches ranging from large cathedrals such as Lewiston's stunning Saints Peter and Paul Church, to tiny missions whose visiting parish priests travel by ferry.

Congregationalism, a Protestant denomination, goes back a long way in Maine. Many of the state's most historic buildings are United Church of

Christ churches, built a century or so ago for town meeting halls as well as places of worship. There are approximately 175 active Congregational Churches in Maine today, including the First Parish Congregational in Brunswick where Martin Luther King, Jr., once preached and Harriet Beecher Stowe regularly worshipped.

The Episcopal Diocese of Maine estimates there are seventeen thousand Episcopalians in the state, worshipping in sixty-eight congregations. Maine's Episcopalians are presided over by Bishop Chilton Knudsen, one of only eleven female bishops (out of six hundred) in the world. Seventeen summer chapels, most of which are found on the coast and islands, are also open for worship in the warmer months.

Maine's Jewish community is small but active. There are approximately twenty synagogues in the state, with more than five hundred families at Portland's Temple Beth El alone. Beth El, located on Deering Avenue, also has a Hebrew school with more than 140 pupils.

Service Organizations

Maine men and women can get involved in a wide range of service organizations, from Rotary International to the American Association of University Women. Here is what's available, for example, in Hancock County alone:

American Legion	Daughters of the
Rotary International	American Revolution
Elks Club	League of Women Voters
Kiwanis Club	Lioness Club
Lions Club	Women's Literary Club
Peace, International	Zonta Club

To research which groups can be found in individual communities, contact area chambers of commerce listed in Appendix 4.

Nonprofit Organizations

In addition to service clubs, scores of nonprofit groups assist causes ranging from protecting Maine's islands to helping victims of AIDS. Maine has branches of national organizations such as Habitat for Humanity and the Make-A-Wish Foundation, as well as nonprofits that are specific to the state.

For example, Maine Island Trail Association volunteers manage recreational use of about eighty public and private islands along more than three hundred miles of coast. Based in Rockland and Portland, the organization was set up to encourage thoughtful, low-impact use of Maine islands. The association depends on volunteers, as do so many worthwhile groups. Again, your local chamber of commerce will know what groups are in your area. (If you'd like more information on the Maine Island Trail Association, contact them at 207-761-8225, or see their website at www.mita.org.)

Retired Senior Volunteer Program (RSVP)

The RSVP program matches volunteers aged sixty and older with community service jobs such as delivering meals, providing companionship to homebound individuals, and teaching in literacy programs. RSVP volunteers also serve at the Maine State Museum, in local schools, libraries, nursing homes, and hospitals. For more information contact:

Aroostook RSVP
P.O. Box 1288
Presque Isle, Me 04769
207-764-3396

Mid Maine RSVP
8 Highwood Street
Waterville, ME 04901
207-873-1127 or 207-626-3430

Mid-Coast RSVP
P.O. Box 808 (43 Park Street)
Rockland, ME 04841
207-596-0361

Southern Maine RSVP
P.O. Box 10480
(307 Cumberland Avenue)
Portland, ME 04104
207-775-6503

RSVP of Eastern Maine
304 Hancock St. Suite 2E
Bangor, ME 04001
207-941-2803

Service Corps of Retired Executives (SCORE)

This organization of volunteers, which is supported by the U.S. Small Business Administration (SBA), recruits retired executives who are interested in utilizing their past experience to counsel people who are starting up small businesses. Volunteers receive travel expenses. For more information contact:

⚑ Augusta SCORE
SBA—Federal Building
40 Western Avenue
Augusta, ME 04330
207-622-8509

⚑ Bangor SCORE
Husson College
Peabody Hall, Room 229
Bangor, ME 04401
207-941-9707

⚑ Central and Northern
Aroostook SCORE
c/o Chamber of Commerce,
P.O. Box 357
Caribou, ME 04736
207-498-6156

⚑ Lewiston-Auburn SCORE
Androscoggin County
Chamber of Commerce
P.O. Box 59
(179 Lisbon Street)
Lewiston, ME 04243-0059
207-782-3708

⚑ Oxford Hills SCORE
215 Main Street
Norway, ME 04268
207-743-0499

⚑ Portland SCORE
66 Pearl Street, Room 210
Portland, ME 04101
207-772-1147

Maine Senior Games

Held in Portland and Bangor, the Maine Senior Games are the state's largest organized competitive event for the fifty-plus members of the population. For information about how you can have fun (and stay fit) by competing in the games, call the Southern Maine Area Agency on Aging, at 1-800-427-7411.

Gardening

Nourishing the soil is another way to nourish one's soul. "If you can garden in Maine, you can garden anywhere," assures the slogan of *People, Places and Plants,* a gardening magazine established in 1996 in Gray. Maine's four growing zones, a frost-free season of—in some years—only one hundred days, and its notoriously rocky soil, might lead people from outside the state to doubt that anything can grow here. What's going to bloom in a place with chilly springs and short—albeit glorious—summers?

"The reality is that Maine has, per capita, the most dynamic horticultural scene in New England," says Paul Tukey, editor and publisher of *People, Places, and Plants.* "Ornamentally, there's extraordinary first-rate gardening going on here, and organic vegetable production is exploding."

The secret to gardening successfully, say veterans, is picking the right plants. "There are so many incredible varieties that are hardy in Maine," says Paul Tukey. "And we have the University of Maine's Horticultural Department, which is possibly the best in New England, plus Johnny's Selected Seeds, in Albion, with the most extensive trial gardens anywhere. Those two institutions take great pains to identify through extensive testing and research what plants will work well here."

Other resources available to gardeners include the University of Maine Cooperative Extension Service, part of an amazing federal network that exists to impart free or low-cost agricultural information to the public (call 207-581-3188 or 1-800-287-0274 to find the office nearest you). And then there are your neighbors, who invariably seem to know the answers to gardening questions.

The length of the growing season depends on several factors. Location is one determinant. Depending on where in the state you garden, you may have a slightly longer growing season and warmer temperatures. Luck is another factor. Killing frosts don't always arrive when the calendar says

autumn. "Some years, we've had gardens blooming from May 1 until mid-October without a frost," says Paul Tukey. "In my book, that's really not a short growing season."

Gardening in Maine has its distinct advantages. For one thing, blooms are more brilliant, due to the

Members of the Camden Garden Club spruce up the Village Green for spring. *Photo courtesy of the* Camden Herald.

197

cooler temperatures and intensity of the growing period. Another bonus is that many pests that plague gardeners in warmer climes can't survive the chilly winters. The cool summer nights are a boon to many plant varieties, and pleasant daytime temperatures and usually reliable rains mean spare time isn't spent watering. Probably the biggest advantage to gardening here, though, is the anticipation of and excitement during the growing season.

"Perhaps because the time is short, Mainers throw themselves into gardening," says Paul Tukey. "I am continually amazed at the quality, quantity, and sheer beauty of Maine's gardens and the incredible talent and dedication of Maine's many gardeners."

POPULAR PLANTINGS

Want to know what Mainers plant? Here are the most popular varieties ordered from Johnny's Selected Seeds in Albion.

ANNUALS
- Dwarf sunflower, *Helianthus annuus*
- Cosmos, *Cosmos bipinnatus*
- Nasturtium, *Tropaeolum majus*
- Sunflower, multi-branching, *Helianthus annuus*
- Painted tongue, *Salpiglossis sinuata*

PERENNIALS
- Lupine, *Lupinus polyphyllus*
- Shasta daisy, *Leucanthemum X superbum*
- Yarrow, *Achillea millefolium*
- Wild Indigo, *Baptisia australis*
- Delphinium hybrid, *Delphinium X belladonna*

VEGETABLES
- Bright lights Swiss chard
- Stringless bush bean
- Stiffneck garlic
- Mild mesclun mix
- Early Nantes carrot

Harvesting flowers at Johnny's Selected Seeds, in Albion.
Photo courtesy of Johnny's Selected Seeds.

Farmer's Markets

The one hundred or so farmer's markets in Maine forge a direct link between consumers and farmers, which means unparalleled freshness. Markets are located throughout the state, and each offers a unique blend of personalities and products.

Here are just a few examples—to find the market nearest you, check out the Department of Agriculture's website at www.mainefood andfarms.com.

⚑ *Portland Public Market.* The newest hot spot in Portland is open every day, year-round. This beautiful new market is located in an award-winning building half a block from Monument Square at Cumberland Avenue and Preble Street. It's an extraordinary resource, full of venders selling farm-fresh foods from across the state. Taste bread warm from the oven, free-range chicken fresh from Deer Isle, buy flowers, spices, fish just off the boat, and listen to entertainment, too. Check www.portlandmarket.com for more information, or call 207-228-2000.

⚑ *Belfast Farmer's Market.* Located at the junction of Routes 1 and 3 in Reny's Plaza, the market features the Bread Box Bakery, Maine-ly Poultry, and Field of Greens, in addition to other farmers and vendors. Open May through October, Tuesday 2:30 to 5:30 PM, and Friday and Saturday 9 AM to 1 PM. Contact www.appletoncreamery.com for more information.

⚑ *Orono Farmer's Market.* Located between College Avenue and the Stillwater River, less than a mile from downtown Orono, at the

University Steam Plant Parking Lot, the Orono market features local produce, maple syrup, jams and jellies, and local crafts. Open every Saturday morning and Tuesday afternoon, May through October, rain or shine.

Public Gardens

Mainers show their enthusiasm for growing things at the more than fifty public gardens maintained by garden clubs and other organizations. Here they are, courtesy of *People, Places and Plants,* listed in roughly geographical order running from south to north.

- *Hamilton House Gardens.* Maine's best example of a Victorian-era garden, this display was recently renovated. South Berwick. 207-384-5269 or 603-436-3205.
- *Laudholm Farm.* The buildings and grounds at this classic saltwater farm offer a glimpse into past seaside farm life, with natural tidal-zone plantings. Wells. 207-646-1555.
- *Grounds and Gardens of St. Anthony's Monastery.* One of the more unusual places to stay in the Kennebunks, St. Anthony's Monastery, has gardens with intriguing pathways and peak rhododendron viewing in June. Kennebunkport. 207-967-2011.
- *Garden at Marrett House.* The restored Victorian gardens here feature an excellent iris collection. Standish. 207-642-3032.
- *Deering Oaks Rose Circle.* The peak bloom of the hybrid tea roses here is during July and early August, when more than 600 species are exhibited. Portland. 207-874-8300.
- *Longfellow Garden.* A Colonial Revival garden, featuring shade plants and color, this lovely spot is on the Congress Street grounds of the Maine Historical Society. Portland. 207-879-0427 or 207-774-1822.
- *Harraseeket Inn Gardens.* One of Freeport's nicest inns, the Harraseeket has an old-fashioned courtyard appearance, and it's ideal for gatherings. Freeport. 207-865-9377.
- *Gardens at Harrington House.* The gardens here include plants from the 1860s, including a 150-year-old lavender. Freeport. 207-865-3170.

▲ *Heather Garden.* This seaside estate near a neat working farm has well-maintained gardens. Wolfe's Neck, Freeport. 207-865-3428.

▲ *Heather Garden at Walker Art Building.* Many hardy heaths and heathers surround Bowdoin's classic art museum. Bowdoin College, Brunswick. 207-725-3000 ext. 3311.

▲ *Coastal Maine Botanical Garden, Inc.* This evolving 128-acre site is the result of an aggressive effort by local citizens to build a premiere garden. Barter Island Road. Boothbay. 207-633-4333.

▲ *Christina's Garden at the Olson House.* Maintained by the Farnsworth Museum in honor of Wyeth family, this garden is named after the subject of the classic American painting, *Christina's World.* Cushing. 207-354-0102.

▲ *Camden Amphitheater.* Escape summer crowds in this classically designed garden by Fletcher Steele. 207-236-3440.

PROFILE

Howard Lupovitch came to Maine in 1998 from Detroit, Michigan, to become the Assistant Professor of Jewish Studies at Colby College. "I'd camped in Acadia a few times as a teenager," he says. "And that was the extent of my time in the state. But both my wife and I grew up in four-season climates, so we were used to winter."

The Lupovitchs are enjoying the hearty lifestyle Maine affords and like living in Waterville. "We're a young couple, just starting out, and we bought a great first house. Plus the people are friendly, the city is clean, and we hardly ever lock a car door," he notes. "We do miss our families, but I like working at Colby very much."

At first, the couple wondered why the state won such high praise. "We enjoyed the summer, but it was in the fall that the magic of Maine really hit us. Our neighbor's tree turned this incredible mixture of yellow and orange, and we looked at each other, and said, 'Ah, Maine—now we get it.'"

Johnny's main trial fields, where everything from astilbe to zucchini is carefully grown. *Photo courtesy of Johnny's Selected Seeds.*

- ▲ *Camden Children's Garden.* A Camden favorite, the children's garden was built in 1996 at the Camden Public Library to honor authors of children's books. Camden. 207-236-3440.
- ▲ *Conway Homestead and Museum.* Known for its historical authenticity, this relatively unknown garden is hidden away in the middle of the tourist Mecca. Camden. 207-236-2257.
- ▲ *Merryspring.* An excellent public reference resource, with improving public grounds, this Camden favorite is a nice place to stroll. Rockport-Camden town line. 207-236-2239.
- ▲ *Gardens of the Castine Inn.* These classic formal gardens sit in a picturesque seaside setting. Castine. 207-326-4365.
- ▲ *Amen Farm Gardens.* Pretty gardens at the home of the late Roy Barrette, garden writer and essayist. Features a newly planted arboretum with 150 uncommon trees. Brooklin. 207-359-8982.
- ▲ *Leighton Sculpture Garden.* The garden at Leighton Gallery is a favorite of many Mainers. Blue Hill. 207-374-5001.

Abby A. Rockefeller Garden. Dazzling interplay of flower beds and sculpture at this private garden, appointment needed. Seal Harbor. 207-276-3330.

Asticou Azalea Garden. Maine's finest Japanese-style garden, with ties to legendary gardener Beatrix Farrand. Northeast Harbor. 207-276-5130.

Beatrix Farrand Garden at College of the Atlantic. One of Acadia's last examples of Farrand's work. Bar Harbor. 207-288-5015.

Thuya Garden. Thuya is noted for its excellent reference library and massive perennial collection. Northeast Harbor. 207-276-5130.

Wild Gardens of Acadia. Twelve different plant habitats at the state's only national park display Maine's native plants. Acadia National Park. 207-288-3338.

Bernard McLaughlin Garden. Famous for its lilacs, the McLaughlin garden was voted the favorite public garden in Maine by the readers of *People, Places and Plants.* South Paris. 207-743-7620.

Gardens of the Blaine House. Originally designed in 1920, the gardens at the Governor's mansion were completed during the 1990s. Augusta. 207-662-6363.

Kennebec Valley Garden Club Park. This Augusta garden is impeccably maintained by one of Maine's most vital garden clubs. Augusta Civic Center, Augusta. 207-622-1124 or 207-622-5227.

Pine Tree State Arboretum. Ornamental trees, an extensive well-labeled hosta collection, and acres of forests distinguish the state's arboretum. Augusta. 207-621-0031.

Johnny's Selected Seeds. Johnny's is home to America's most extensive trial gardens for vegetable seedlings, and it also has herbs and flowers. Albion. 207-437-9294.

Fay Hyland Botanical Plantation. Affiliated with the University of Maine, this botanic collection features hardy plants native to Maine. Orono. 207-581-2978.

Gardens of Brewster Inn. Designed by architect John Calvin Stevens in the 1930s for a former Maine governor, these beds have been updated by local innkeepers. Dexter. 207-924-3130.

Conclusion

It's been nearly fifteen years since I bid farewell to Boston and made the journey Down East. Those years have been a rich time for me: I married, bought my first house, found friends, welcomed three children into the world, and launched several businesses. I've climbed Mount Katahdin, driven an ambulance, and listened to loons on a still lake. I have snowshoed by moonlight and watched a deer swimming in the surf. Some of these events might have happened no matter where I lived; many occurred because I live in Maine.

Writing this book has caused me to reflect on people and things connected to my state, and it has proven to be a wonderfully affirming experience. Mainers are working hard to preserve what is so special about this place, while at the same time creating a better future for young and upcoming generations. There is much to be done, but also much for which to be thankful.

I have particularly enjoyed hearing the comments of newcomers, many of whom express the same sentiments I felt years ago. Their observations prompted me to see the state anew, helped me gain a fresh appreciation of Maine's gifts, and gave me a sense of gratitude for the graceful twists of fate that brought me here in the first place.

When you cross the Piscataqua River to become more than a visitor to Vacationland, I know you will receive a warm welcome. Then the tiller will be in your hands, and your unique talents and gifts will be needed. Good luck—and smooth sailing.

V.W.D.

Acknowledgments

I'd like to thank all of the new Mainers who shared their experiences with me: Elizabeth Burrell and Gary Swanson, Lynda and Thad Chilton, Gordon Cox and Carol Doherty-Cox, Barry Hurtt, Jay Culberth and Lynn Johnson, Marlene Kinlin, Jan and David Njaa, Bill and Allie Lou Richardson, Mary Griffin, Brad Rourke and Andrea Jarrell, Dorothy Paradis, Peter Mahncke, Howard Lupovitch, Kristine and Jason Scher, Howard Jones, and Bob and Laurie Price. Some of these folks I met in the oddest places—on the Islesboro ferry or at the local preschool—and some I spoke to only by phone or on-line, yet all were gracious with their time and comments.

I'm grateful to all of the good folks locally and around the state who helped with my research, in particular Eric Von Magnus at the State Planning Office, and Kirk Mohney, of the Maine Historic Preservation Commission. Thanks also to all of the individuals and organizations who so graciously allowed me to reprint their photographs. As with most things in Maine, when asked, people went out of their way to be helpful.

With each writing project I do, I am amazed by the knowledge and kindness of Maine's librarians, and I thank in particular my friends at the Camden Public Library. I appreciate the support of the great folks in the midcoast region, natives and transplants alike, especially my running, hiking, and book club buddies. Grateful thanks to my allies Nancy Albertson and Kathy Merrill, for lending a hand when I faced both a bored daughter and a pressing deadline, and to my patient pal Tom Ford for his timely computer consulting. I have enjoyed working with Neale Sweet, Karin Womer, and Andy Vietze at Down East Books—thank you all for your expertise and patience with a first-timer. Kudos to Janet Patterson for designing such a beautiful book. And thank you, Mom, for your bold decision to move to Maine, which prompted me to write this book in the first place.

Finally, thank you to my family, especially Ed—the best editor, counselor, cook, and cheerleader a writer could have.

APPENDIX 1:
Maine at a Glance

Data provided by *Down East* magazine.

County	Androscoggin	Aroostook	Cumberland	Franklin
Population 1996*	101,754	78,113	251,087	29,200
Population 1990	105,259	86,936	243,135	29,008
Population 1980	99,509	91,344	215,789	27,447
Largest Town (1996 pop.)	Lewiston 36,830	Presque Isle 9,213	Portland 63,123	Farmington 7,883
People per square mile	226	13	294	16
High School Graduates	71.8%	70.9%	85%	79.7%
College / Adv. Degree	12.6%	12.5%	27.6%	17.7%
Median Household Income	$26,979	$22,230	$32,286	$24,432
Aver. Temp. Range, °F	Lewiston	Caribou	Portland	Farmington
January	29.2 to 11.1	19.4 to –1.6	30.3 to 11.4	25.8 to .5
April	53.1 to 34.2	46.7 to 29	52.3 to 34.1	51 to 28.5
July	80.7 to 60.7	76.5 to 54.5	78.8 to 58.3	79 to 53.4
October	59 to 40.5	52 to 34	58.7 to 38.3	57.4 to 32.3
Crime Rate per Thousand (1998)	39	19	39	35

----

* Most recent census estimate.

Maine At A Glance, continued

County	Hancock	Kennebec	Knox	Lincoln
Population 1996*	49,500	116,214	37,487	31,303
Population 1990	46,948	115,904	36,310	30,357
Population 1980	41,781	109,889	32,941	25,691
Largest Town (1996 pop.)	Ellsworth 6,292	Augusta 20,441	Rockland 7,905	Waldoboro 5,248
People per square mile	33	132	100	68
High School Graduates	83.3%	78.9%	80.8%	81.4%
College / Adv. Degree	21.4%	18.1%	19.8%	22.2%
Median Household Income	$25,247	$28,616	$25,405	$28,373
Aver. Temp. Range, °F	Ellsworth	Augusta	Rockland	Wiscasset**
January	30.1 to 10.5	27.6 to 10.4	32 to 10.2	30.1 to 10.4
April	51.7 to 32.3	52.1 to 34.4	n/a	52.4 to 34.2
July	77.9 to 57	79 to 60.1	79.9 to 57.1	77.9 to 59.3
October	57.8 to 39.3	57.5 to 39.8	n/a	58.4 to 39.4
Crime Rate per Thousand (1998)	27	27	21	16

---

* Most recent census estimate.
** Based on the average temperatures at Brunswick, the nearest National Weather Service station.

Maine At A Glance, continued

County	Oxford	Penobscot	Piscataquis	Sagadahoc
Population 1996*	53,797	144,989	18,329	35,508
Population 1990	52,606	146,601	18,653	33,535
Population 1980	49,043	137,015	17,634	28,795
Largest Town (1996 pop.)	Rumford 6,880	Bangor 31,649	Dover-Foxcroft 4,272	Bath 10,026
People per square mile	27	45	5	142
High School Graduates	76.9%	79.1%	75.4%	81.1%
College / Adv. Degree	12.7%	17.7%	12.3%	21.6%
Median Household Income	$24,535	$26,631	$22,132	$31,948
Aver. Temp. Range, °F	Rumford	Bangor	Dover-Foxcroft	Bath**
January	27.2 to 5.8	26.7 to 8.2	24.2 to 2.4	30.1 to 10.4
April	52.3 to 31.2	50.9 to 32.8	49.5 to 28.8	52.4 to 34.2
July	79.6 to 56.4	78.1 to 58.3	78.6 to 54.5	77.9 to 59.3
October	57.5 to 36.6	56.9 to 38.7	55.6 to 33.6	58.4 to 39.4
Crime Rate per Thousand (1998)	28	33	26	26

---

* Most recent census estimate.
** Based on the average temperatures at Brunswick, the nearest National Weather Service station.

Maine At A Glance, continued

County	Somerset	Waldo	Washington	York
Population 1996*	52,507	35,822	36,224	171,482
Population 1990	49,767	33,018	35,308	164,587
Population 1980	45,049	28,414	34,963	139,739
Largest Town (1996 pop.)	Skowhegan 9,790	Belfast 6,474	Calais 3,915	Sanford 20,801
People per square mile	14	49	14	173
High School Graduates	71.9%	77.4%	73.2%	79.5%
College / Adv. Degree	10.5%	16.8%	12.7%	19%
Median Household Income	$22,829	$23,148	$19,993	$32,432
Aver. Temp. Range, °F	Madison	Belfast	Eastport	Sanford
January	26.8 to 2.1	32 to 10.7	29.7 to 13.9	32.5 to 10.4
April	51.2 to 30.1	53.9 to 32.3	48.5 to 32.8	57.3 to 32
July	79.1 to 55.6	79.9 to 57.1	72.9 to 53	83.2 to 57.1
October	57.2 to 34.7	59.9 to 38.9	55.7 t0 40.8	62.5 to 37.1
Crime Rate per Thousand (1998)	33	14	23	31

* Most recent census estimate.
** Based on the average temperatures at Brunswick, the nearest National Weather Service station.

APPENDIX 2:
Quality Medical Care—Maine Hospitals

Data provided by *Down East* magazine.

Note: Numbers in parentheses following hospital names indicate number of acute care beds in that facility.

Augusta

Maine General Medical Center *(142)*
6 East Chestnut St., Augusta, ME 04330
207-626-1000

Bangor

Acadia Hospital *(100)*
P.O. Box 422, Bangor, ME 04402-0422
207-973-6100

Eastern Maine Medical Center *(411)*
P.O. Box 404, Bangor, ME 04402-0404
207-973-7000

St. Joseph Hospital *(100)*
360 Broadway, Bangor, ME 04401
207-262-1000

Bar Harbor

Mount Desert Island Hospital *(49)*
P.O. Box 8, Bar Harbor, ME 04609-0008
207-288-5081

Belfast

Waldo County General Hospital *(45)*
P.O. Box 287, Belfast, ME 04915
207-338-2500

Blue Hill

Blue Hill Memorial Hospital *(26)*
Water St., Blue Hill, ME 04614
207-374-2836

Biddeford

Southern Maine Medical Center *(150)*
P.O. Box 626, Biddeford, ME 04005
207-283-7000

Boothbay Harbor

St. Andrews Hospital *(22)*
P.O. Box 417,
   Boothbay Harbor, ME 04538
207-633-2121

Bridgton

Northern Cumberland Memorial
   Hospital *(40)*
P.O. Box 230, Bridgton, ME 04009
207-647-8841

Brunswick

Mid-Coast Hospital *(145)*
58 Baribeau Dr., Brunswick, ME 04011
207-729-0181

Parkview Hospital *(55)*
329 Maine St., Brunswick, ME 04011
207-729-1641

Calais

Calais Regional Hospital *(49)*
50 Franklin St., Calais, ME 04619
207-454-7521

Quality Medical Care—Maine Hospitals, continued

Caribou

Cary Medical Center *(65)*
163 Van Buren Rd., Caribou, ME 04736
207-498-3111

Damariscotta

Miles Memorial Hospital *(32)*
Bristol Rd., Damariscotta, ME 04543
207-563-1234

Dover-Foxcroft

Mayo Regional Hospital *(46)*
75 West Main St.,
    Dover-Foxcroft, ME 04426
207-564-8401

Ellsworth

Maine Coast Memorial *(64)*
50 Union St., Ellsworth, ME 04605
207-667-5311

Farmington

Franklin Memorial Hospital *(70)*
1 Hospital Dr., Farmington, ME 04938
207-778-6031

Fort Kent

Northern Maine Medical Center *(52)*
143 East Main St., Fort Kent, ME 04743
207-834-3155

Greenville

C.A. Dean Memorial Hospital *(14)*
P.O. Box 1129, Greenville, ME 04441
207-695-2223

Houlton

Houlton Regional Hospital *(49)*
20 Hartford St., Houlton, ME 04730
207-532-9471

Lewiston

Central Maine Medical Center *(250)*
300 Main St., Lewiston, ME 04240
207-795-0111

St. Mary's Regional Medical
    Center *(233)*
P.O. Box 291,
    Lewiston, ME 04243-0291
207-777-8100

Lincoln

Penobscot Valley Hospital *(25)*
Box 368, Transalpine Rd.,
    Lincoln, ME 04457-0368
207-794-3321

Machias

Down East Community Hospital *(38)*
RR 1, Box 11, Machias, ME 04654
207-255-3356

Millinocket

Millinocket Regional Hospital *(42)*
200 Somerset St.,
    Millinocket, ME 04462
207-723-5161

Norway

Stephens Memorial Hospital *(50)*
181 Main St., Norway, ME 04268
207-743-5933

Pittsfield

Sebasticook Valley Hospital *(28)*
99 Grove Hill, Pittsfield, ME 04967
207-487-5141

212

Quality Medical Care—Maine Hospitals, continued

Portland

New England Rehabilitation
  Hospital (100)
335 Brighton Avenue,
  Portland, ME 04102
207-775-4000

Maine Medical Center (606)
22 Bramhall St., Portland, ME 04102
207-871-0111

Mercy Hospital (200)
144 State St., Portland, ME 04101
207-879-3000

Presque Isle

Aroostook Medical Center (105)
Box 151, Academy St.,
  Presque Isle, ME 04769
207-768-4000

Rockport

Penobscot Bay Medical Center (109)
6 Glen Cove Dr.,
  Rockport, ME 04856-4240
207-596-8000

Rumford

Rumford Community Hospital (49)
420 Franklin St., Rumford, ME 04276
207-364-4581

Sanford

Goodall Hospital (49)
25 June St., Sanford, ME 04073
207-324-4310

Skowhegan

Redington–Fairview General
  Hospital (65)
P.O. Box 468, Skowhegan, ME 04976
207-474-5121

South Portland

Spring Harbor Hospital (106)
175 Running Hill Rd.,
  S. Portland, ME 04106
207-761-2200

Waterville

Inland Hospital (46)
200 Kennedy Memorial Dr.,
  Waterville, ME 04901
207-861-3000

MaineGeneral Medical Center
  (Seton and Thayer units) (202)
30 Chase Ave., Waterville, ME 04901
207-872-1000

Westbrook

Westbrook Community Hospital (30)
40 Park Rd., Westbrook, ME 04092
207-854-8464

York

York Hospital (66)
15 Hospital Dr., York, ME 03909
207-363-4321

APPENDIX 3:
Local Issues—Maine Newspapers

Data provided by *Down East* magazine.

DAILIES

Augusta

Kennebec Journal
274 Western Avenue,
  Augusta, ME 04332
207-623-3811

Bangor

Bangor Daily News
P.O. Box 1329, Bangor, ME 04402
207-990-8000

Biddeford

Journal Tribune
P.O. Box 627, Biddeford, ME 04005
207-282-1535

Brunswick

The Times Record
P.O. Box 10, Brunswick, ME 04011
207-729-3311

Lewiston

The Sun-Journal
P.O. Box 4400, Lewiston, ME 04243
207-784-5411

Waterville

Central Maine Morning Sentinel
31 Front Street, Waterville, ME 04901
207-873-3341

Portland

Portland Press Herald
P.O. Box 11350, Portland, ME 04104
207-791-6650

Maine Sunday Telegram
P.O. Box 11350, Portland, ME 04104
207-791-6650

WEEKLIES AND OTHERS

Augusta

Capital Weekly
P.O. Box 2788, Augusta, ME 04338
207-621-6000

Bangor

The Weekly
P.O. Box 2237, Bangor, ME 04402
207-942-2913

Bar Harbor

The Bar Harbor Times
P.O. Box 68, Bar Harbor, ME 04609
207-288-3311

Bath

Coastal Journal
P.O. Box 705, Bath, ME 04530
207-443-6241

Belfast

Republican Journal
P.O. Box 327, Belfast, ME 04915
207-338-3333

The Waldo Independent
P.O. Box 228, Belfast, ME 04915
207-338-5100

Bethel

The Bethel Citizen
P.O. Box 109, Bethel, ME 04217
207-824-2444

Biddeford

Biddeford–Saco–Old Orchard Beach Courier
P.O. Box 1894, Biddeford, ME 04005
207-282-4337

Blue Hill

The Weekly Packet
P.O. Box 646, Blue Hill, ME 04614
207-374-2341

Boothbay Harbor

The Boothbay Register
P.O. Box 357,
   Boothbay Harbor, ME 04538
207-633-4620

Brewer

Maine Times
P.O. Box 969, Brewer, ME 04412
207-991-9640

Bridgton

The Bridgton News
P.O. Box 244, Bridgton, ME 04009
207-647-2851

Bucksport

The Enterprise
P.O. Box 829, Bucksport, ME 04416
207-469-6722

Calais

The Calais Advertiser
P.O. Box 660, Calais, ME 04619
207-454-3561

Camden

The Camden Herald
56 Elm Street, Camden, ME 04843
207-236-8511

Cape Elizabeth

The Cape Courier
P.O. Box 6242,
   Cape Elizabeth, ME 04107
207-767-5023

Caribou

Aroostook Republican & News
P.O. Box 608, Caribou, ME 04736
207-496-3251

Castine

Castine Patriot
P.O. Box 205, Castine, ME 04421
207-326-9300

Cutler

The Downeast Coastal Press
HCR 69 Box 287, Cutler, ME 04626
207-259-7751

Damariscotta

Lincoln County News
P.O. Box 36, Damariscotta, ME 04543
207-563-3171

Lincoln County Weekly
P.O. Box 1287,
    Damariscotta, ME 04543
207-563-5006

Dexter

The Eastern Gazette
P.O. Box 306, Dexter, ME 04930
207-924-7402

Dover-Foxcroft

Piscataquis Observer
P.O. Box 30, Dover-Foxcroft, ME 04426
207-564-8355

Eastport

The Quoddy Tides (twice monthly)
P.O. Box 213, Eastport, ME 04631
207-853-4806

Ellsworth

The Ellsworth American
P.O. Box 509, Ellsworth, ME 04605
207-667-2576

The Ellsworth Weekly
P.O. Box 1122, Ellsworth, ME 04605
207-667-5514

Farmingdale

Community Advertiser
324 Main Avenue,
    Farmingdale, ME 04344
207-582-8486

Farmington

Franklin Journal (twice weekly)
P.O. Box 750, Farmington, ME 04938
207-778-2075

Fort Fairfield

Fort Fairfield Review
128 Main St., Suite 7,
    Ft. Fairfield, ME 04742
207-472-3111

Gray

The Gray News
P.O. Box 433, Gray, ME 04039
207-657-2200

Greenville

Moosehead Messenger
P.O. Box 400, Greenville, ME 04441
207-695-3077

Houlton

Houlton Pioneer Times
P.O. Box 456, Houlton, ME 04730
207-532-2281

Islesboro

Islesboro Island News (six per year)
P.O. Box 104, Islesboro, ME 04848
207-734-6921

Kennebunk

York County Coast Star
P.O. Box 979, Kennebunk, ME 04043
207-985-2961

Kingfield

The Irregular
P.O. Box 616, Kingfield, ME 04947
207-265-2773

Lincoln

Lincoln News
P.O. Box 35, Lincoln, ME 04457
207-794-6532

Livermore Falls

Livermore Falls Advertiser
P.O. Box B,
   Livermore Falls, ME 04254
207-897-4321

Lubec

The Lubec Light
R.R. 2, Box 380, Lubec, ME 04652
207-733-2939

Machias

The County Wide
P.O. Box 497, Machias, ME 04654
207-564-7548

Machias Valley News Observer
P.O. Box 357, Machias, ME 04654
207-255-6561

Madawaska

Saint John Valley Times
P.O. Box 419, Madawaska, ME 04756
207-728-3336

Millinocket

Katahdin Times
P.O. Box 330, Millinocket, ME 04462
207-723-7090

Milo

The Town Crier
P.O. Box 158, Milo, ME 04463
207-943-7384

New Gloucester

New Gloucester News
P.O. Box 102, New Gloucester, ME
04260
207-926-4036

Norway

Advertiser Democrat
P.O. Box 269, Norway, ME 04268
207-743-7011

The Bear Facts (twice monthly)
P.O. Box 718, Norway, ME 04268
207-583-2851

Old Town

Penobscot Times
P.O. Box 568, Old Town, ME 04468
207-827-4451

Portland

Casco Bay Weekly
561 Congress Street,
   Portland, ME 04101
207-775-6601

Presque Isle

The Star-Herald
P.O. Box 510, Presque Isle, ME 04769
207-768-5431

Rangeley

Rangeley Highlander
P.O. Box 542, Rangeley, ME 04970
207-864-3756

Rockland

The Courier Gazette (three/week)
P.O. Box 249, Rockland, ME 04841
207-594-4401

The Free Press
6 Leland Street, Rockland, ME 04841
207-596-0055

Rumford

Rumford Falls Times
P.O. Box 490, Rumford, ME 04276
207-364-7893

Sanford

The Sanford News
P.O. Box D, Sanford, ME 04073
207-324-5986

Skowhegan

Somerset Gazette
P.O. Box 887, Skowhegan, ME 04976
207-474-0606

South China

The Town Line
P.O. Box 89, South China, ME 04358
207-445-2234

Stonington

Island Ad-Vantages
P.O. Box 36, Stonington, ME 04681
207-367-2200

Westbrook

The American Journal
4 Dana Street, Westbrook, ME 04092
207-854-2577

Windham

The Suburban News
733 Roosevelt Trail, Windham, ME
04062
207-892-1166

Wiscasset

Wiscasset Newspaper
P.O. Box 429, Wiscasset, ME 04578
207-882-6355

York

The York Weekly
P.O. Box 7, York, ME 03909
207-363-4343

APPENDIX 4:
Chambers of Commerce

Data provided by the Maine Office of Tourism.

[Augusta]
Kennebec Valley Chamber of Commerce
P.O. Box 676, Augusta 04332-0676
207-623-4559

Bangor Region Chamber of Commerce
519 Main Street, Bangor 04402-1443
207-947-0307

Bar Harbor Chamber of Commerce
P.O. Box 158, Bar Harbor 04609
207-288-5103

[Bath]
Chamber of Commerce of the
    Bath–Brunswick Region
45 Front Street, Bath 04530
207-443-9751

Belfast Area Chamber of Commerce
P.O. Box 58, Belfast 04915
207-338-5900

Bethel Area Chamber of Commerce
P.O. Box 1247, Bethel 04217
207-824-2282

Biddeford–Saco Chamber of Commerce
110 Main Street, Suite 1202,
    Saco 04072
207-282-1567

[Bingham]
Upper Kennebec Valley Chamber
    of Commerce
P.O. Box 491, Bingham 04920
207-672-4100

Boothbay Region Information Center
P.O. Box 187, Boothbay 04537
207-633-4743

Boothbay Harbor Region
    Chamber of Commerce
P.O. Box 356, Boothbay Harbor 04538
207-633-2353

[Bridgton]
Greater Bridgton Lakes Region
    Chamber of Commerce
P.O. Box 236, Bridgton 04009
207-647-3472

[Brunswick]
Chamber of Commerce of the
    Bath–Brunswick Region
59 Pleasant Street, Brunswick 04011
207-725-8797

Bucksport Bay Area
    Chamber of Commerce
P.O. Box 1880, Bucksport 04416
207-469-6818

Calais Regional Chamber of Commerce
P.O. Box 368, Calais 04619
207-454-2308

Camden–Rockport–Lincolnville
    Chamber of Commerce
P.O. Box 919, Camden 04843
207-236-4404

Caribou Chamber of Commerce
111 High Street, Caribou 04736
207-498-6156

Sugarloaf Area Information Center
RR 1 Box 2151,
   Carrabassett Valley 04947
207-235-2100

Damariscotta Region
   Chamber of Commerce
P.O. Box 13, Damariscotta 04543
207-563-8340

Damariscotta Region
   Information Bureau
P.O. Box 217, Damariscotta 04543
207-563-3175

[Dover-Foxcroft]
Southern Piscataquis County
   Chamber of Commerce
P.O. Box 376, Dover-Foxcroft 04426
207-564-7533

Eastport Area Chamber of Commerce
P.O. Box 254, Eastport 04631
207-853-4644

Ellsworth Area Chamber of Commerce
P.O. Box 267, Ellsworth 04605
207-667-2617

[Farmington]
Greater Farmington
   Chamber of Commerce
RR 4 Box 5091, Farmington 04938
207-778-4215

Fort Fairfield Chamber of Commerce
128 Main Street, Suite 4,
   Fort Fairfield 04742
207-472-3802

[Fort Kent]
Greater Fort Kent Area
   Chamber of Commerce
P.O. Box 430, Fort Kent 04743
207-834-5354

Freeport Merchants Association,
P.O. Box 452, Freeport 04032
207-865-1212

[Greenville]
Moosehead Lake Region
   Chamber of Commerce
P.O. Box 581, Greenville 04441
207-695-2702

Houlton Chamber of Commerce
109 Main Street, Houlton 04730
207-532-4216

[Island Falls]
Northern Katahdin Valley Regional
   Chamber of Commerce
P.O. Box 374, Island Falls 04747
207-463-2077

Jackman–Moose River Region
   Chamber of Commerce
P.O. Box 368, Jackman 04945
207-668-4171

Kennebunk–Kennebunkport
   Chamber of Commerce
P.O. Box 740, Kennebunk 04043
207-967-0857

[Kittery]
Gateway to Maine
P.O. Box 526, Kittery 03904
207-439-7545

[Lewiston]
Androscoggin County
   Chamber of Commerce
P.O. Box 59, Lewiston 04243-0059
207-783-2249

Limestone Chamber of Commerce
291 Main Street, Limestone 04750
207-325-4025

220

Lincoln Chamber of Commerce
P.O. Box 164, Lincoln 04457
207-794-8065

Machias Bay Area
Chamber of Commerce
P.O. Box 606, Machias 04654
207-255-4402

[Madawaska]
Greater Madawaska
Chamber of Commerce
378 Main Street, Madawaska 04756
207-728-7000

Maine Chamber and Business Alliance
7 University Drive, Augusta 04330-9412
207-623-4568

[Millinocket]
Katahdin Area Chamber of Commerce
1029 Central Street, Millinocket 04462
207-723-4443

Naples Information Center
P.O. Box 412, Naples 04055
207-693-3285

Mount Desert Chamber of Commerce
P.O. Box 675, Northeast Harbor 04662
207-276-5040

Ogunquit Chamber of Commerce
P.O. Box 2289, Ogunquit 03907
207-646-2939

Old Orchard Beach
Chamber of Commerce
P.O. Box 600, Old Orchard Beach 04064
207-934-2500

[Portland]
Convention and Visitors Bureau of
Greater Portland
305 Commercial Street, Portland 04101
207-772-5800

Presque Isle Area
Chamber of Commerce
P.O. Box 672, Presque Isle 04769
207-764-6561

Rangeley Lakes Region
Chamber of Commerce
P.O. Box 317, Rangeley 04970
207-864-5571

Rockland–Thomaston Area
Chamber of Commerce
P.O. Box 508, Rockland 04841
207-596-0376

[Rumford]
River Valley Chamber of Commerce
P.O. Box 598, Rumford 04276
207-364-3241

St Francis Chamber of Commerce
P.O. Box 123, St Francis 04774
207-398-3431

Sanford-Springvale
Chamber of Commerce and
Economic Development
261 Main Street, Sanford 04073
207-324-4280

Skowhegan Area
Chamber of Commerce
P.O. Box 326, Skowhegan 04976
207-474-3621

Oxford Hills Chamber of Commerce
P.O. Box 167, South Paris 04281
207-743-2281

Southwest Harbor–Tremont
Chamber of Commerce
P.O. Box 1143,
Southwest Harbor 04679
207-244-9264

Deer Isle–Stonington
    Chamber of Commerce
P.O. Box 459, Stonington 04681
207-348-6124

[Unity]
Waldo County Regional
    Chamber of Commerce
P.O. Box 577, Unity 04974
207-948-5050

[Van Buren]
Greater Van Buren
    Chamber of Commerce
65 Main Street, Van Buren 04785
207-868-5059

Waldoboro Town Office
P.O. Box J, Waldoboro 04572
207-832-5369

[Waterville]
Mid-Maine Chamber of Commerce
P.O. Box 142, Waterville 04903-0142
207-873-3315

Wells Chamber of Commerce
P.O. Box 356, Wells 04090
207-646-2451

Wilton Chamber of Commerce
P.O. Box 934, Wilton 04294
207-645-3932

Windham Chamber of Commerce
P.O. Box 1015, Windham 04062
207-892-8265

Yarmouth Chamber of Commerce
158 Main Street, Yarmouth 04096
207-846-3984

Yorks Chamber of Commerce
571 US Route 1, York 03909
207-363-4422

Appendix 5:
Retirement Communities

Every year more retirement communities are being built or expanded. Please call or write the individual facilities for their latest information. (Data as of March 2000, provided by *Down East* magazine.)

The communities listed here all provide housekeeping services and at least one meal per day, and most can provide transportation.

Key to abbreviations in the Types of Units column:
IA = independent apartments; C = cottages;
A = Alzheimer's units; LT = long-term care beds;
AL = assisted living units.

FACILITY	Number of Residents	Distance to Hospital	Rent, Purchase or Both	Types of Units
Auburn				
Clover Health Care 440 Minot Ave., Auburn, ME 04210 207-784-3573 www.mainecare.com	270	3	R	IA, AL, LT, A
Schooner Retirement Community 200 Stetson Rd., Auburn, ME 04210 207-784-2900; 800-924-9997 www.schoonerestates.com	180	3	R	IA, AL, LT
Augusta				
Granite Hill Estates P.O. Box 187, Augusta, ME 04332 207-626-7786; 888-321-1119 www.granitehillestates.com	150	2	B	IA, C, AL
Bangor				
Park East Retirement Villa 146 Balsam Dr., Bangor, ME 04401 207-947-7992	16	1	R	IA

FACILITY	Number of Residents	Distance to Hospital	Rent, Purchase or Both	Types of Units
Bangor, cont.				
Boyd Place	n/a	n/a	R	IA
21 Boyd St., Bangor ME 04401				
207-941-2837				
Belfast				
Penobscot Shores	73	.25	B	IA, C
10 Shoreland Dr., Belfast, ME 04915				
207-338-2332				
www.wchi.com/penobscot_shores.html				
Blue Hill				
Parker Ridge Retirement Community	70	3	B	IA, C, AL
HC 64, Box 270, Blue Hill, ME 04614				
207-374-5789				
www.parkerridge.net				
Boothbay Harbor				
St. Andrews Village	150	.75	B	IA, C, AL, LT, A
145 Emery Lane, Boothbay Harbor, ME 04538				
207-633-0920				
www.standrewsvillage.com				
Brewer				
Ellen M. Leach Memorial Home	66	1.5	R	IA
P.O. Box 359, Brewer, ME 04412				
207-989-6352				
Brunswick				
Thornton Oaks	200	.1	P	IA, C, AL
25 Thornton Way #100, Brunswick, ME 04011				
207-729-8033; 800-729-8033				
www.thorntonoaks.com				

FACILITY	Number of Residents	Distance to Hospital	Rent, Purchase or Both	Types of Units
Camden				
Camden Gardens	10	5	R	IA, C
110 Mechanic St., Camden, ME 04843				
207-236-0154				
Cape Elizabeth				
Chancellor Gardens	40	4	R	AL
78 Scott Dyer Rd., Cape Elizabeth, ME 04107				
207-799-7332; 888-860-6914				
www.carematrix.com				
Damariscotta				
Schooner Cove	55	.1	B	IA
65 Schooner St., Damariscotta, ME 04543				
207-563-5523				
www.mileshealthcare.org/schooner				
Falmouth				
OceanView at Falmouth	175	6	P	IA, C, AL, A
52 Falmouth Rd., Falmouth, ME 04105				
207-781-4460				
www.oceanviewrc.com				
Farmington				
Orchard Park Rehabilitation and Living Ctr.	12	5	R	IA, AL
12 North St., Farmington, ME 04938				
207-778-4416				
Gorham				
Gorham House	170	12	R	IA, AL, LT, A
50 New Portland Rd., Gorham, ME 04038				
207-839-5757				
www.mainecare.com				

FACILITY	Number of Residents	Distance to Hospital	Rent, Purchase or Both	Types of Units
Hampden				
Avalon Village	15	4	B	IA, C
50 Foxglove Dr., Hampden, ME 04444				
207-862-5100				
www.avalon-maine.com				
Houlton				
Madigan Estates	135	1.5	R	IA, AL, LT, A
93 Military St., Houlton, ME 04730				
207-532-6593				
www.madiganestates.com				
Kennebunk				
Atria Kennebunk	60	7	R	AL, A
1 Penny Ln., Kennebunk, ME 04043				
207-985-5866				
Huntington Common	155	4.5	R	IA, C, AL, A
1 Huntington Com. Dr., Kennebunk, ME 04043				
207-985-2810; 800-585-0533				
www.huntingtoncommon.com				
The Farragut at Kennebunk	40	2.5	P	IA, C
71 Portland Rd., Kennebunk, ME 04043				
207-985-0300; 877-985-0300				
www.thefarragut.com				
Lewiston				
Montello Heights	60	2	R	IA
550 College St., Lewiston, ME 04240				
207-786-7149				
Portland				
Seventy-Five State Street	185	.1	R	IA, AL
75 State St., Portland, ME 04101				
207-772-2675				

FACILITY	Number of Residents	Distance to Hospital	Rent, Purchase or Both	Types of Units
Portland, cont.				
The Atrium at Cedars 640 Ocean Ave., Portland, ME 04103 207-775-4111 www.atriumatcedars.com	60	2.5	P	IA
The Park Danforth 777 Stevens Ave., Portland, ME 04103 207-797-771 www.parkdanforth.com	160	4	R	IA, AL
Presque Isle				
Leisure Gardens Apartments 4 Dewberry Dr., Presque Isle, ME 04769 207-764-7322 www.ainop.com/lgardens/	89	.1	R	IA, AL
Rockland				
Bartlett Woods 20 Bartlett Dr., Rockland, ME 04841 207-594-2745 www.bartlettwoods.com	45	2	B	IA, C
Saco				
Wardwell Retirement Neighborhood 143 Middle St., Saco, ME 04072 207-284-706 www.wardwell.org	102	2.5	R	IA, AL
Scarborough				
Piper Shores (scheduled completion 2001) 27 Baxter Blvd. Portland ME 04101 207-772-9090; 888-333-8711	160	12	life care	IA, C, AL, LT, A

FACILITY	Number of Residents	Distance to Hospital	Rent, Purchase or Both	Types of Units
Topsham				
The Highlands 26 Elm St., Topsham, ME 04086 207-725-2650; 888-760-1042 www.highlandsrc.com	325	2.5	B	IA, C, AL, A
Waterville				
Park Residences 141 West River Rd., Waterville, ME 04901 207-861-5685 www.woodlandsalf.com	115	1	R	IA, AL, A
Winslow				
Winslow Place 361/2 Garand St., Winslow, ME 04901 207-877-7064; 800-876-9212 www.bridgesbiz.com	19	1.5	R	IA
Yarmouth				
Bay Square at Yarmouth 27 Forest Falls Dr., Yarmouth, ME 04096 207-846-0044 www.benchmarkquality.com	50	10	R	IA, AL, A
York				
Sentry Hill 2 Victoria Ct, York, ME 03909 207-363-5116 www.sentryhill.com	125	.12	B	IA, C, AL, LT, A
Spring Pond Estates 284 York St., Rt. 1A, York, ME 03909 877-351-8444 www.springpondestates.com	20	1.5	P	C, AL

Index

▲▲ Look for these other guides ▲▲
From Down East Books

Spring Wildflowers of New England and *Trees and Shrubs of New England*
by Marilyn Dwelley
   Marilyn Dwelley's indispensable field guides are truly user-friendly. Information on range, habitat, appearance, and growth habit is complemented by hundreds of detailed color illustrations. Hardcover books bound in water resistant Hyflex®.
Spring Wildflowers, 224 pages
Trees and Shrubs, 276 pages

The Guide to Maine Golf Courses
by Park Morrison, editor & copublisher of *TravelGolf Maine* magazine
   All the key information for more than 120 public courses: locations, facilities, green fees, tee-off details, and course descriptions, including slope and USGA ratings, along with course histories and profiles of the more interesting holes. Color photos.
Paperback, 168 pages

A Birder's Guide to Maine
The Definitive Handbook for Inland and Coastal Birding
by Elizabeth and Jan Erik Pierson, and Peter Vickery
   The complete resource for Maine birding. Clear maps and directions guide birders to the best sites. Loaded with specific information on where and when certain species are likely to be seen, including the fall and spring migrations. Maps.
Paperback, reinforced binding, 400 pages

Maine's Most Scenic Roads
25 Routes Off the Beaten Path
by John Gibson
   Tune up the car or pump up the bike tires and take a spin with John Gibson, author of many hiking and walking guides to New England. This is a selection of particularly scenic and enjoyable routes on the quieter back roads. Photos and maps.
Paperback, 192 pages

**Check your bookstore for Down East's many
other books of Maine interest.**

**Catalog available by calling 1-800-766-1670,
or visit www.downeastbooks.com.**